MW01678913

I CHING

Translated and Interpreted by
Bobby Klein, Ph.D.
Foreword by Mark Hyman, M.D.

Copyright 2021 © by Bobby Klein
ISBN: 978-0-578-83191-6

All rights reserved. Printed in the United States of America. No part of this book may be reproduced or utilized in any form or by any means, electronic or mechanical, including photocopying, recording, or by any information storage and retrieval system, without permission in writing from the publisher.

To correspond to the author of this book or to subscribe to his free I Ching Weekly readings delivered to your in-box, contact bobbyk@bobbyklein.com, or visit his website: www.bobbyklein.com.

Tulum Publishing
1880 Century Park East
Suite 200
Los Angeles, Ca. 90067
310-663-9366

TULUM
PUBLISHING

CONTENTS

Foreword by Mark Hyman, M.D. *vii*
Introduction *xi*
Consulting the I Ching Oracle *xix*
Table of 64 Hexagrams *xxi*

1. Qian	Creation/Inspiration/Dragon *1*
2. Gui Mei	Receptive and Yielding *5*
3. Zhun	Sprouting *8*
4. Meng	Without Experience *12*
5. Xu	Attending *16*
6. Song	Dispute/Conflict *19*
7. Shi	The Collective *23*
8. Pi	Union *27*
9. Xiao Chu	The Small Accumulating *32*
10. Lü	Mating with the Tiger *35*
11. Tai	Peaceful Prosperity/Heaven on Earth *39*
12. Pi	Decline/Stagnation *43*
13. Tong Ren	Harmonizing People *46*
14. Da You	Possession in Great Measure *49*
15. Qian	Humbling *53*
16. Yu	Enthusiasm *57*

17. Sui Following/Adapting *61*
18. Gu Decay/Corruption/Repair *64*
19. Lin Nearing/Letting Go *67*
20. Guan Overseeing/Observing *71*
21. Shi He Biting Through *75*
22. Bi Adorning/Refining *79*
23. Po Splitting Apart *82*
24. Fu Returning *85*
25. Wu Wang Disentangling *88*
26. Da Chu Great Accumulation *91*
27. Yi Nourishment/Tiger's Mouth *95*
28. Da Guo The Great Exceeding *98*
29. Kan The Pit/Danger *102*
30. Li Radiance/Auspiciousness *105*
31. Xian Conjunction *108*
32. Heng Persevering *112*
33. Dun Retiring *115*
34. Da Zhuang Great Power *119*
35. Jin Flourishing *123*
36. Ming I Hiding the Light *127*
37. Chia Jen The Group *131*
38. Kui Polarizing *134*
39. Jian Obstruction/Difficulties *138*
40. Xie Unraveling *142*
41. Sun Diminishing and Offering *145*
42. Yi Augmenting/Blessings in Great Measure *149*
43. Guai Deciding/Parting *152*
44. Guo Coupling *156*
45. Ts'ui Gathering Together *160*
46. Sheng Ascending *163*

47. Kun Confinement *166*
48. Ching The Well *170*
49. Ge Skinning/Revolution *174*
50. Ding The Sacred Vessel *177*
51. Zhen The Rousing *181*
52. Gen Bound/Coming to Stillness *184*
53. Jian Gradual Advance *187*
54. Gui Mei Subordinate/Converting *191*
55. Feng Abundance/Fullness *194*
56. Lu The Wanderer *197*
57. Sun The Gentle *201*
58. Dui The Open/Joyful Expression *205*
59. Huan Dispersion *209*
60. Jie Articulating/Boundaries *212*
61. Chung Fu Inner Truth/Influence *216*
62. Xiao Guo Small Movements/Bird in Flight *219*
63. Ji Ji Already Crossing *223*
64. Wei Ji Correct Order/Missing Pieces *227*

Acknowledgements *231*
About Bobby Klein *233*

FOREWORD

On my bookshelf sits the yellowed, weathered copy of Richard Wilhelm's 1950 translation of *The I Ching or Book of Changes,* the ancient text of Chinese wisdom, a book of oracles and divination that has guided me for over forty years. The language is obtuse, its meanings often obscure and tied to a different time and culture, but within it lies timeless wisdom and guidance for humanity, for each of us yearning to know the truth underneath the unexplainable and answers to the questions of being human. In this fresh translation by Bobby Klein, access to the wisdom contained in the ancient text, communicated in language that is current, relevant, and accessible, is finally available to a new generation.

Every Sunday morning, a gift comes to my email in the form of a reading from the I Ching, to read or to listen to as read with heart by Klein. Within it there is resonance, nuggets of truth and wisdom that seem eerily relevant to this moment, to the questions arising in my life, to the subtext of my subconscious, creating an illuminated framework for navigating life. These readings are precious, alive, prescient, relevant, and curiously portentous. They lift the heart, free the mind, and open the soul to the unseen, dimly known rhythms of the world. I have traveled with Bobby Klein along this road, intersecting with his wisdom and kindness for many years, dipping into his well of understanding in moments of confusion or curiosity. Just as I have focused my life on relieving suffering through functional medicine and by making sense of the complexities of our human biology, Bobby has been on a journey of relieving suffering through soul healing for decades.

As a young man, my heart and mind were called to the exploration of consciousness, seeking to understand the nature of things, witnessing in the fabric of my life the synchronicity of people and events. Life seemed to arise from something unexplainable by our senses or by science—except for quantum physics, which mirrors the discoveries of ancient explorers of inner space. These strange coincidences hinted at laws of consciousness that I felt only dimly. I studied Buddhism and Taoism, poured myself into ancient texts, including the I Ching, for clues; I went to mountains and rivers and oceans, went to meditation retreats, sat at the feet of Zen masters and the Dalai Lama, yogis and healers, trying to sort through the universal questions of meaning, of finding a way to listen to what is often only faintly heard in the din of our modern world.

Ancient traditions often provide tools to see through the cracks, to open doorways to the mind and soul and to what Carl Jung called the *collective unconscious,* the invisible web of interconnected consciousness and energy that flows through all of us. The I Ching is one of those important tools we can use to divine that which is true within our experience, to help us dip into our deeper knowing, to wake up to what is real and true in the moments of our life, dark or light.

Some turn to tarot, or psychics, or numerology, or other esoteric practices, which are difficult to access or understand. In this simple, clear, accessible translation of the I Ching, the culmination of a lifetime's study, of a life that has been the vehicle for transmitting this ancient wisdom, we now have a wide-open doorway to the ancient wisdom of this nearly prehistorical text first written on cuneiform stones. It offers a way for us to access our truths, to bring light to the unconscious or shadow side, which is more relevant now than ever before. Each of us has a higher inner voice, a deep wisdom often buried in the busyness of life. The I Ching helps us access that, but it also brings in a larger wisdom, a wisdom that exists out of time and space, a wisdom that is universal and that connects us all to one another and to all the teachings and pregnant possibilities of our existence. A friend once told me that "coincidence is God's way of staying anonymous." In a way, the I Ching makes it a little less anonymous.

The New Earth I Ching is an indispensable companion for each of us in this turbulent time. Within it are nuggets of wisdom that are intensely relevant to each of us, and signposts that can serve as guidance for all of us in these stormy times. I am grateful for the clarity, dedication, and gift of this book for the ages.

Mark Hyman, MD
Head of Strategy and Innovation
Cleveland Clinic Center for Functional Medicine
September 2020

INTRODUCTION

Traditional teachings have long pointed to a time such as what we face today, as the old story of our world ends. Amid the collapsing structures that have held the old ways in place for millennia, it is said that a golden age will arise. As the old systems collapse, the energy they contain is being released in a powerful and turbulent flow of chaos—the precursor of a new energetic form taking shape here on Earth, for as Sun Tzu says, "In the midst of chaos there is also opportunity." We all sense this monumental archetypal shift in the present historical moment.

The new paradigm on the rise is being led by the power of the Divine Feminine, which is not to be found in outer realities, but only by going deep within and coming to know oneself. It is here that we encounter our mastery as we connect to the presence of the Divine within us. It is here that we confront the outer chaos, ride the big wave of rising consciousness, and learn how to be the wings of the butterfly as we shape our reality. In the emerging model, we discover that the linear, mechanistic model of time gives way to *timing,* a spiral of creative power that is found only in the present moment, where we are co-creators with the Divine.

The I Ching, or Book of Changes, charts the spiraling flow of yin and yang, feminine and masculine, inner and outer energies, revealing glimpses into the higher order of the universe. It is also a book of Taoist philosophy that offers guidance as to proper conduct and procedure as we make our way through this human journey and come into conscious, co-creative alignment with Earth's new harmonic. The sixty-four hexagrams, or *kua,* are all possibilities, archetypes circulating within our individual and collective being at any given time. By going into stillness and invoking the power of divine wisdom, our awareness is brought to bear on those aspects of ourselves—mental patterns, habits, persistent thought forms—that create feelings of separation. The timing of any given I Ching hexagram holds the key to our liberation from the belief in an inauthentic self and opens our path to experiencing our truth: union with the Divine, Oneness. At this time, when we may ask ourselves *How can I, a mere person, effect the global shift of the ages?* The answer is quite simple: by connecting with one's inherent Divine presence, the I AM, the source of all wisdom, healing, and creative transformation.

My Journey with the I Ching

In the 1960s, in Los Angeles, California, the I Ching was very popular in my milieu. It was a dynamic time of change that, fractal-like, reverberates today, and even louder. We were seekers and revolutionaries back then, Whole Earth Catalog dreamers searching for meaning in life and a way forward through the morass. I would refer to the I Ching whenever I was at a crossroads. As other methods of sortilege come into my world, I became entranced by the tarot and numerology as well. I was then introduced to the art of divination by shells in an African ritual shown to me by West African writer Meladoma Patrice Somé.

Years passed, and my career path became a winding road that

took me to studying and eventually becoming certified in Jungian psychology. Jung was fascinated with Buddhist and Taoist thought and methods and studied the I Ching. As I proceeded in my life and practice, the I Ching became more than just a tool; it was a study and a devotion, and I began to use it in my counseling practice. I used the classic Wilhelm Baynes translation, a scholarly tome and the only translation available in the West at the time. As it was when I first began using the I Ching for guidance on my personal path and now in my practice, I found it to be rather obtuse and difficult for my Western mind to find my way into the depth of the spiritual, psychological, and cosmic meanings of the hexagrams, or kua. Nevertheless, I would use the kua as a way of introspection for my consultations with patients. I didn't throw coins, the traditional method; I would simply open the book to a page at random, knowing, of course, that there is nothing random in the universe—there is guidance and assistance from unseen forces who are always with us.

I had been a student of Taoism, and my path brought me to the study of acupuncture and Traditional Chinese Medicine, and I became one of the first licensed practitioners of this ancient medical art. My teacher introduced me to tai chi, and I was a second-level teacher for many years. I mention this because all of these sinological studies gave me a feeling for Taoism, for the writings of Confucius, and for the wisdom of the poetic Tao Te Ching, the bedrock of Taoist philosophy. More and more I found the Baynes translation of the I Ching that I had been using to be steeped in thoughts that I felt were behind the times. The language was sexist and the references to relationships, politics, and business were old ideas and not very useful.

I began to search for a copy of the I Ching, or *Yi Jing,* as the earliest form of this oracle is known, that was as close to the original as I could possibly find. History says that the I Ching dates back eight or nine thousand years. This was before the advent of written language, so it was for a long time an oral transmission that was passed down from master to student. As written language came into practice in the time of the Chou Dynasty (1150–249 BCE), annotations of the sixty-four hexagrams came into use. In my search for a translation that would resonate in modern times, and with the help of Professor Wen Shen Wang, a well-regarded scholar and Sinologist, I was presented with a copy in old Chinese cuneiform that was said to be 1500 years old. It had been copied many times, and I received it as a faded mimeograph. This is the text I began to use and still use to this day. At that point I had only a rudimentary understanding of Chinese that I had gained in my study of Traditional Chinese Medicine and acupuncture, so Professor Wang and a linguist colleague of his helped me translate the sixty-four hexagrams.

What I found, to my delight, was that the I Ching is not only lyrical, it is also quite modern in its universal language. I began to use my new translation of the sixty-four hexagrams in my practice as a therapist with my patients as well as for myself. I had the notion to access the ancient wisdom and send it out as a weekly reading to a few of my patients, as email was just coming into existence. The list began to grow and grow, and it now it includes tens of thousands.

This brings me to this volume. It is my translation—with a lot of help—and my interpretation of the hexagrams. The Book of Changes is an invaluable resource as we awaken to the incredible opportunity being offered to humanity during this time of chaos, as the planetary energy system shifts to a higher order of coherency in its journey to a new energetic state. We are being put on notice that our lives can no longer be taken up in duality and conflict, which both individually and collectively slows us down and causes us to lose our connection to the life force. We are each of us and all of us in a cosmic dance with the new frequencies, whether we know it or not, and those of us committed to planetary evolution must be in clear intention and focus as to what we create in the New Earth.

Though I Ching translates as "Book of Changes," I think of it more as a book of answers, answers to questions about how to take action (or refrain from action) and which way to turn to bring success and good fortune, while acting as a conscious co-creator. The oracle advises the user as to which road to take to find happiness, especially when you are feeling muddled or blocked; it also points to the path of the greater good, where the individual and the collective intersect. Using this book is a practice, and as with any practice the more time you invest in its study the more useful it becomes.

Consider that we are all part of the universe, and there is universal energy abounding constantly in our lives, what in Chinese medicine is known as *chi* or *qi*. The I Ching as a living oracle gives voice to this energy. There truly is a consciousness to the universe. The esoteric principle "As Above, So Below" says that we contain the universe and all its possibilities in our individual selves. And just as the universe wants us to continue in the best and most whole way possible, the I Ching tells us that all is perfect, and our path is as well. Yes, there are obstacles and dangers. But with the proper use of the oracle's wisdom these obstacles become opportunities for lessons learned. We learn that by joining with the universal archetypal patterns as recorded in the Book of Changes, we discover that we live in an endless Now. And our progress, healing, and enlightenment depend on living fully in the Now, as there there is no past and no future, as quantum physics shows us. There is only the wholeness of a beautiful Now.

If we accept that all of our creations and ideas have been channeled from the universe, we have a better understanding of this book. The key, or access, is not outside of us. It exists within us as a language of the soul, the guiding force of which human incarnation is only one aspect. The space of the soul is where we enter into a kind of archeological dig to uncover what we have hidden from ourselves that keeps us from experiencing oneness with all, a state of bliss. It is a place of profound peace of mind and trust. Once entered, it is a sacred space where anything and everything is possible. In stillness, through prayer and meditation, we can hear this voice of wisdom. With this oracle we are reassured that this voice is meant for each of us and always aims for the greater good.

There are many ways to access the river of universal knowledge. There is the tarot, astrology, yarrow sticks, and shells, all of which can lead us to interpreting the timing of our lives and receive the information necessary to continue in the most graceful and loving way possible. We all have questions that can be answered as to whether to act, retreat, or delay. This is the essence of the strategy of moving toward a life of harmony, abundance, and love. Knowing this, we can gain the confidence to ask the right questions of the I Ching and receive its coded message. The message will be heard differently by each querent of the oracle. The magic is that we hear it or read it in a way that tells us how, when, and why we are to act or not act on the situation before us.

The Chinese emperor and sage Fu Hsi developed a system of inquiring the I Ching in the form that we use today. There are sixty-four hexagrams, or kua, and each represents a situation or condition relating to the particular stage of evolution. By taking the appropriate action, we can turn any situation into the most beneficial outcome under the circumstances.

Make no mistake, your questions will be answered! There is no doubt about this as you will receive guidance to live a better and more whole life, one in harmony with the universe and the flow of cosmic energy, the Tao. You will be guided not only on the correct action, but also on the best attitude to adopt as you move forward to obtain a particular result. Old patterns that serve you no longer will be removed, and you will be advised on what to discard and what to replace old ideas and actions with, and how. In following the advice of the oracle you will be counseled as to how to be a whole person, a person of honesty, integrity, and compassion, the place of the soul. You may be advised to confront evil if it is at your door, but fear not—the oracle will walk you through step-by-step to a place of safety and sanctity.

Note well that the universe is perfect, and we as its spawn are perfect as well. To align with our full human potential, the direction and advice from a cosmic source of wisdom outside of our little selves is on offer. This is what the I Ching is all about.

I wish you well on this journey, and I am humbled and honored to bring this text to you.

—Bobby K

CONSULTING THE I CHING ORACLE

Traditionally, the I Ching was consulted by throwing fifty yarrow stalks, a rather complex but deeply engaging process that engages the querent in a ritual that helps maintain the proper mindset. This book outlines a more common method of inquiry, one that can be done much more easily while preserving the proper ritual feeling of the traditional method.

After clearing your mind and adopting the proper attitude of openness while holding a question in your thoughts or simply maintaining an open state, ready to receive the oracle's guidance on your current state, take three coins of the same type, such as three pennies. The coins are thrown six times, one throw for each line in the hexagram.

To calculate the lines from the coins thrown, values are assigned to the coins' sides:

Heads/yang = 3	solid line ———
Tails/yin = 2	broken line — —

Even totals (6 or 8) are given the value of a yin, broken line, while odd totals (7 or 9) are given the value of a yang, solid line. The values of the three coins are added to get the total to determine the line. The hexagram is built from the bottom up, so the first line is the bottom one, the sixth line the top one.

A word on changing lines:

Many translations and instructions for the use of the I Ching use changing lines as determined by coins (6 and 9 are designated as changing lines, which change from yin to yang or the other way around). The resulting hexagram that is formed by means of the changing lines forms a second hexagram, which is paired with the original hexagram (note that the I Ching does not predict the future, so the new hexagram formed is not a prophecy). I do not use changing lines in my method. I like to keep it simple and believe this was the original way of consultation. I have studied the I Ching for many years and have not been able to find the exact origin of the idea of changing lines. Therefore, when I use coins, I use the simple method of no changes. There are other methods. When I studied with one of my teachers, Dr. Robert Girard, he would come to stillness and just open the book; wherever it opened was always sage advice. I find this, too, to be a wonderful method, as there is nothing arbitrary in the universe when there is a meeting of time, intent, and one's state of being. This is synchronicity, a concept of *timing* that contrasts with the more static, linear concept of *time.* In the New Earth paradigm, timing replaces the old way of looking at time.

The I Ching is a ritual that you do not want to rush. I like to light some incense and find a quiet place. Come to stillness and meditate on your question, and ask the oracle to give you the wisdom you need in answer to your query. When you're ready, shake the three coins in your cupped hand and release onto a flat surface or on a cloth you use as part of your ritual for this purpose. Each throw gives you a line. Once you've completed six throws and determined your hexagram, use the chart in this book to locate the oracle's number and message.

The items you use for this ritual should be respected. The bag of tiles should be placed in a sacred spot. Or, if using coins, try to use the same six coins each time and wrap them in a silk cloth or place in some other container after use.

The more you use the I Ching, the clearer the answers are. You will become adept at understanding what the oracle is telling you about correct behavior and attitude in relation to your question.

The Table of 64 Hexagrams

	☰	☳	☵	☶	☷	☴	☲	☱
☰	1	34	5	26	11	9	14	43
☳	25	52	3	27	24	42	21	17
☵	6	40	29	4	7	59	64	47
☶	33	62	39	52	15	53	56	31
☷	12	16	8	23	2	20	35	45
☴	44	32	48	18	46	57	50	28
☲	13	55	63	22	36	37	30	49
☱	10	54	60	41	19	61	38	58

1. QIAN CREATION/INSPIRATION/DRAGON

䷀

Above Qian Heaven
Below Qian Heaven

The wisdom

This kua signals a blessing from Heaven.
Confucius says that when Heaven blesses us
It helps us, and to be helped by Heaven
Is to be helped indeed.

Spirit helpers have brought you to the gates of creation, the creation of you or the creation of an idea or project. Now as you pass through the gates where you will shift into an accelerated timing of passion and inspiration, there is an accessible force to call on. It is the dragon force within. This dragon, the signifier of raw kundalini energy, is your ally and helper and offers the gift of creative power and persistence. Persistence is necessary as you begin a new cycle of manifestation and transformation.

The energy received is a primal force that is emerging from the depths of your soul. It will transform and ultimately obliterate previous obstacles. With proper consideration and respect for the combined forces of spirit and consciousness, you will come into harmony with the rhythm of Gaia, the living Earth force in all her sacred glory. Should you not stay in your integrity you would miss out on this rare blessing. Look inward to see where you have not been clear with yourself or others. If so, this kua says no blame—simply correct your thinking and actions. Now is the time to gain insight into what is to be joined with and what shall be torn asunder. Obstacles old and new are now appearing in multitudinous forms. These challenges come because you have chosen to walk in the light of divine consciousness.

As this primal source of strength emerges, so does the ego, hungry for this power and tempting you with motives of self-interest, control, or greed. If your ego attempts to use this energy of inspiration and creativity to activate base thoughts or negative words or deeds, immediately correct your course, as this would certainly bury you in the depths of despair, and you would be cast out of the very gates you have worked so hard to pass through, causing you to repeat the same old lessons again until you come into harmony with the universal laws. Therefore, the benefit now is to give up the front you've been using as a defense. It will serve you no more.

Having Qian show at this time requires diligence and an unceasing belief in yourself and the work that is before you now. Examine your motives for the success you seek. Be certain that it is for your highest good as well as the greater good of all. Recognize your own habitual thoughts and reactive behaviors, the demons of your past that have been fed by guilt and shame. Make a concerted effort to correct and replace these old, outworn patterns with positive thoughts and actions. Consider that the words you think—about yourself or others—are more powerful and have a greater effect than the words you speak.

Now is the time to enter into the frequency of expanded consciousness that is being presented by the blessings of Qian.

> You have been hoping
> For clarity to be revealed;
> With a considered strategy
> Now is the time to
> Put your plans into action.

From deep within comes the mystical force that bridges the world of unseen forces and the material, rather confusing world of our collective reality. Call on this primordial dragon force that is now available to you, and you will ease into a higher wisdom, the wisdom of the ancestors. However, keep in mind that tapping into this dragon energy will be dangerous if you are not in harmony with your own inner truth and in balance with the correctness of the times. So stay in truth no matter what challenges or obstacles you face. The right projects and relationships will stay, and where there is doubt, greed, or ego, they will quickly fade. In all worldly matters, invoke your strength by accessing—and trusting—your intuition, which is the doorway to a higher wisdom. In so doing, you will be in line with the universal laws. Above all, stay in humility before the dragon, which comes through you but does not originate with you.

To have arrived at the gates of this new and abundant cycle means that you have done your work. In this cycle you will find the proper way to think and act. As you move forward, keep your eyes clear, remain sober, and commit to the greater good. In business as in personal matters let go of any thoughts or judgments that disparage or limit others. Refrain from using negative generalities about the opposite sex or those who are in a different flow of life, and instead invoke thoughts and words of compassion. Take the high road and be a light-bearer, especially now, when so many people are consumed by darkness in the form of greed, abuse, and fear. In this way you will not chase away the grace and abundance that you have long desired.

There is a very real possibility that during this cycle of inspiration you will become stressed or tired as you move forward. There is much to do in times like these, so take the time you need to relax, rejuvenate, and have fun with friends and family. You are the shining light now. Share your light and positive vibes with those around you, be they friends or fellow pilgrims, and even strangers. Raise the vibration around you. Never have the times been more ready for us to be of service to the greater good while we honor Gaia.

There is a saying that is the essence of the teaching of this hexagram: keep your eyes on the stars and your feet on the ground. In this way you will be able to give and receive unconditional love.

2. GUI MEI RECEPTIVE AND YIELDING

Above Zhen — shake, excite, inspire
Below Dui — open, free, unhindered

The wisdom

Give way to the teachings of others;
Work with purpose and gusto;
Walk with fellow pilgrims who align with you and your view;
Do not lead—follow.

Consider the traditional Chinese story of the maiden who has married and is invited into the clan of her new husband. The benefit is for her to listen and observe and not make waves. This is not weakness; it is yielding and shows a willingness to follow the ideas and rituals of a new family and environment. In this way she will know what to expect and how to become a part of the tapestry of her new life situation while maintaining her dignity and composure.

This is a metaphor for your situation now as you approach a new position, whether in life or in love. Be still and bend with the wind—not the winds of fate, but the winds of change. In this way your strength will become manifold.

Be in your truth without any fanfare, and in this place of humility your rightful place will emerge. If you try to be the outspoken truth-talker now your words will not be heard; they will be construed as negative and counterproductive, even though you know they aren't. Overt action would cause you to lose the opportunity to join with those who have, for the right reasons, chosen you.

This is a time of initiation.
It is a precarious time.
You are on the brink of joining with others
To move forward.
For now remain still.

You are in a well-deserved state of grace. This is the time to deconstruct what in the past may have been ego-based actions. These actions, if repeated now, would create obstacles in your movement toward the greater good, taking you off the mark of finding peace and well-being. To show your light and wisdom now would be seen as a threat, and you would be prevented from joining the family, relationship, group, or tribe you desire and that desires you. As hard a pill as it may be to swallow, be subordinate. This will allow you to see the inner workings of the situation, where many truths are hidden from view. If, prodded by the voice of the ego, you were to bluster your way in without doing the work of following the path of self-knowledge, the quiet path, you would be rebuked; truths would not be revealed, the road you have carefully tread to get to this point would be blocked, and you would be sent back to begin anew. This can be a prosperous cycle provided you adhere to correctness and not worry about what others think of you.

Although you have learned and experienced much in moving toward your goal, you still need to acquire a deep, even mystical knowledge of the situation so that at the proper time you can step up and have the kind of influence that will bring the relationship, business, or tribe into a beneficial position. It is from this reserved stance that you will influence your journey toward your goals, as you will be in harmony with the frequencies of the greater good, for yourself and your fellow pilgrims. For now, metaphorically bow your head while you determine the lay of the land. Once you've passed through this cycle you'll be able to raise your head and shine the brilliant light you have held in your heart.

Forewarned is forearmed! Chill. Bide your time. It won't take long. Quiet the ego, contemplate, and meditate.

> Know well your long-range plans.
> In the quiet of contemplation
> Silently make your plans.
> Your time of influence is not yet.

Not yet does not mean never. It means that the energies are not properly aligned for you to influence the situation at this time. Be content to be a part of the nameless crowd or a member of the team who works diligently but does not try to show any special greatness or cleverness. It is from this position that you will observe where there are dangers and pitfalls. In this way you will become a secret agent of the soul, so that when you make your move into the inner sanctum of your desires you do so with ease, style, and grace. This will be the dance you have long desired, the dance of love that nourishes life.

Lessons of humility and compassion are contained in this hexagram. This will eventually lead to the harvest. So, be inconspicuous—but that doesn't mean you should not laugh and dance. Do so, definitely! And be here now, fully present. You are in no danger; your protection is your stillness and in following. This kind of response will notify those around you and the universe that you are happy to bide your time. There is great power in this signification, and in singing and praying every day. Your voice will please Spirit. Sing with no judgment of good or bad; just be fully in your song and prayer.

3. ZHUN SPROUTING

Above Kan precipice, danger
Below Zhen arouse, excite, inspire

The wisdom

The beginning of a new cycle has arrived.
It wears no disguise.
It is real, tender, delicate, and vulnerable
Just as you are now.

A seed you planted in the past and almost forgot has sprouted. As it rises from the depths of your soul's memory it comes to you laced with excitement and passion. Along with its emergence is a feeling of confusion, a confusion that has resulted from this surprise appearance.

As with many new ventures, the way forward is not absolutely clear; you cannot yet see it, but you can *feel* it. It is this lack of clear vision as to outcomes that is causing some befuddlement about how to move forward, what or who to let go of, and what to nurture and protect during this cycle of new growth. Do not let any emotions you are feeling take you off-track. Muster all your energy and call on your hidden strengths by accessing your intuition. You are being called on to change your way of thinking about what is real and what is fantasy. It is here that your intuition will be at its zenith; as long as you trust it, you will move beyond any doubts or fears.

Your hopes, skills, and desires have all joined to awaken this new cycle. Be gentle with yourself and protect this delicate and vulnerable beginning by gathering your strength through an uncompromising examination of your truth. This new cycle has begun because of your past hard work and your having let go, knowingly or not, of expectations. In fact, this is the magic of creation: no expectations. Because you didn't cloud your vision by projecting a future outcome, you fertilized the ground for this seed of passion, creativity, and love to spring forth.

As you gather your strength, look into the areas of your being where you have the most self-confidence. From this point of view tap into your higher wisdom by accessing your intuition. Intuition is the gateway to the Divine. Call it what you will—your guides, teachers, or the angels. Whatever name you give it, it is here for you now, to tune into and follow. In trusting this voice of wisdom you will be safe and on the mark. If you feel confused, gather your courage, dip into your inner sage, or reach out to a wise person in your tribe to assist you in sorting out the messages. Once you make your approach to the sage, have respect; listen to and act on what you hear. In this way you will keep your channels fully open.

Thunder and rain
Are coming simultaneously.
It is loud and difficult to hear.
Listen to the thunder
And seek shelter from the rain.

You are experiencing the birth of something new. However difficult and dangerous a birth it may be, it is the birth of a new perspective, a new way of thinking that will allow you to persevere and succeed. Perseverance in facing the coming thunderstorm of activity will deliver abundance and joy, which will lead to a brilliant outcome.

With new growth comes unfamiliar risks. Mate your intuition

with your courage. Pause for a moment and reflect, and then make your move. Many things are in seeming disarray around you. Friendships, relationships, and the inner workings of your community and tribe are all trying to find their balancing point. Let them be and do not try to fix anything; you have new growth to attend to. While digging deep into your intuitive self, these situations will reconcile on their own without your interference. In fact, were you to step away from this period of new growth to deal with the confusion around you, you would prevent those situations from finding their natural order, and the potential for an abundant harvest presented by the timing of this kua would likely slip away from you while you were busy grasping at straws.

Stand your ground. There will surely be obstacles on your path, but these are temporary, like a thunderstorm that comes, shakes the ground, and then moves on, leaving moist, fertile soil that has been prepared to birth the new. In humility see your place between Heaven and Earth and realize that with this new cycle comes nourishment of your inner being and an evolution of your spirit and self. Align with the greater good, for yourself and others, and the way will be made clear and imbued with meaning.

In business, find gifted helpers to work with and advise you. In your personal relationships, communicate openly and with a fresh approach to the truth you see and feel. Take counsel with trusted friends or teachers. In this way you will protect this new growth, this fresh new plan, with the understanding gained from experiencing your own vulnerability. This will lead you to the place within, where love resides.

This time may well be felt as a difficult rite of passage, and it is. It will require diligence and patience, especially patience with yourself. Remember, what comes easily usually doesn't last. Your magic will be found in your ability to make a relationship with any difficulties you face and disassemble. In this way what has sprouted will grow and bring an abundant harvest.

If risk is your ally, let fear be your fuel. What you hear is the call to your warrior self to protect your creations, feelings, and ideas, which will carry you gracefully into the cycle opening up before you. You are blessed, so be grateful and raise your sword of truth to any obstacle that comes your way.

All is in perfect order as we face this exciting shift of the ages. Trust that it is real. Call for it, embrace it, and it will be yours in a shower of love and abundance.

4. MENG WITHOUT EXPERIENCE

䷃

Above Ken mountain, firm-rooted, nothing to lose
Below K'an water, fast-flowing, possible danger

The wisdom

Go to the wise teachers.
You will be a gift to them.
The joy and purpose of the elders and teachers
Is to teach.

You are entering new territory. It is wise to approach those who have gone before you who are a repository of wisdom. Follow tradition as you make your approach and admit that you have little or no experience in the situation before you. Then, in humility, ask for guidance. Listen respectfully and only ask again if you did not understand. It is permissible to ask for clarity.

You may well be the teacher who will be approached to give counsel. Respect your questioner and honor the strength it took for them to make the approach, then dispense your knowledge. If you are not heard or understood, do not change your stance. Hold firm, for as time passes, the universe will allow the student to absorb the lessons.

What is stirring in you has many layers and great depth. Be aware that some aspects are hidden and will only be accessed in your dedication to finding stillness; be it for a few minutes, a day, or longer, no matter—it's your intention that counts. Don't try to make it appear that you know what you don't. To know the unknowable, come to what in Zen is called *shoshin,* "beginner's mind." It refers to cultivating an attitude of openness, eagerness, and a lack of preconceptions, just like a beginner; this is especially applicable if you are already at an advanced level.

> The stillness of the mountain is not still at all;
> Water springs from the rocks in the mountain,
> nourishing all beings,
> To become a river flowing to the sea.
> This is the springtime of youthful beginnings
> and experiences;
> A youthful attitude brings boundless success.

You are well-positioned now to accept that at this point in your life you know not how to proceed. Revel in the beginner's feeling of newness. Listen to the voice of your Higher Self, reached in the silence of a quiet mind. Reach out and ask for advice from a mentor, a wise friend, an elder in the tribe. In making your approach in humility, offer alms of respect and gratitude. Consider the advice given and go within, into the quiet of your heart.

Adopting the mindset of a young student, the attitude of the beginner, will serve you well. Be as still and calm as the mountain and allow the coming flow of knowing to spring forth. The knowledge you need will at first be like water dripping through the rocks. With care, confidence, and integrity, this subtle outpouring will in time become a magnificent flowing river that carries your dreams of love and abundance to the ocean of completion. In this way you will fill in the gaps in your knowledge, to be carried to a peaceful and joyous conclusion.

All of us have unseen teachers and guides who are wise, patient, and kind. You are now at the place where you can hear their voices and feel their compassion and love.

Often the question arises, "How do I connect?" The answer is in this kua: be open, without any preconceptions. Express wonder for another day upon awakening, when you see the beauty of nature, when you hear the songs of the birds. Strive to be an innocent, in awe of all that is new.

In your youth it seemed that summer would never come, and a year was such a long time. As we got older, a year seemed like a moment, and our youth seemed to have slipped away. It has not. All that's happened is that we've become "sophisticated" and complacent, thinking we already know so very much. This hexagram comes to help you return to that state of childlike wonderment of the new. Be still and learn what is to be learned if you are the student. Be still and listen if you are the mentor, guide, or teacher.

Complacent, you've become dull to the love all around you. This has caused loneliness and frustration. Therefore, in your relationships, projects, or on your own inner journey of conscious evolution it will be of great benefit to refresh your attitude. You must think in a new way about how things are showing up in your life. Quiet the ego and move into your inner knowing, your intuitive force that never disappoints. Then when you come to the realization that you do not have enough knowledge to proceed, something wonderful will happen: you will become the student again, the beginner who is filled with wonder.

Recall what brought you joy and what you did for fun as a child and do it now. Skip, play with clay, steal a kiss, finger-paint. Whatever it is, reignite your innocence and sense of wonder. If as a child you were traumatized around trust or love, accept that it happened, write about it, process it, and let it go. Move into a different pool of conscious activity, one that is joyous and filled with gratitude.

We are in revolutionary times, and the revolution is one of

consciousness. An open mind and heart will see you through this passage. Trust love, be love, and return to the bubbling well of youthful enthusiasm, tempered by a clear and meditative mind.

5. XU ATTENDING

䷄

Above Kan gorge, test, a critical time, tread with caution
Below Qian/Gan Heaven, energy, Spirit power

The wisdom

You have made the approach
Toward manifestation.
Now, waiting with patience is key.
Success will come as you nourish that which needs attention.

Look to your spirit and transform yourself into a great cat in the wild, crouching, waiting for the opportune time to make your move. While waiting, look to the things you have developed as if they were your clowder, being sure to protect them and not ignore them. See to the needs of your projects, relationships, family, and tribe, and keep them close and well-looked-after, well-nourished. Remain steadfast during this period of waiting for the correct time to seize the opportunities that are close by, so close you can feel them but cannot as yet see them.

Waiting is necessary on the path to attainment. While you wait, know that the waiting will end and the needed nourishment will come. Impatience shows weakness and a lack of trust. Fate is at hand. Have the inner strength to roll with fate and bide your time. This will allow all the elements to align in perfect order. Any faltering at this time sours the water and makes toxic any nourishment that may come. So be light of heart. By understanding that this is fate, you will avoid any precipitous actions that would cause delays. Have confidence that with proper and considered action you are moving toward the greater good.

One of the most difficult aspects of the human condition is waiting with grace and dignity. When we conceive a project or enter a relationship, we glimpse our desired outcome. Much time is spent making plans and doing the footwork to bring about that outcome. Then, for no obvious reason, the movement toward our goal is stopped or put on hold. This brings frustration and angst. It is precisely at this moment that you will benefit from making a relationship with the concept of waiting.

In business, be confident of success and be open to change. If you're in a worrisome relationship, be patient; it will improve by growing or changing. If you aren't in a relationship but long for one, know that it will come in its own sweet time as you, in your crouching pose of catlike waiting, follow your heart while letting go, so that change will seem like a holiday.

The elements to embrace while waiting:
Dignity
Integrity
Compassion
Kindness

Waiting is not time wasted. Xu advises us to cultivate a joyful heart during this time. Make it a ceremonial time, a time to look inward. Quiet the analytical mind and change the inner voicings of doubt and fear to words of love and correctness. This paves way for nourishment to arrive.

Traditional cultures did not just sit around and worry when the rain didn't come to nourish their fields. They went into ritual, ceremonies that included rain dances, gifts to the gods, and expressions of gratitude for what they already possessed. And it worked.

And if the rain did not come, changes were made. Crops were moved or changed, and the creative force came without effort or thought, it just was. All understood that the people themselves were not in charge, nor were the shamans and priests. The defining component was the belief that by uniting with Spirit and the ancestors, life would be renewed. The people's confidence in the unity of seen and unseen forces fueled the joy of the collective, the community. So it is for you. Do your ceremonies; give yourself the gifts of patience and tempered merriment. This will fill the void and allow you to wait with the proper intention to receive. While waiting, closely examine your strategic moves. Eliminate what isn't necessary. Travel light. This will make the waiting more pleasurable and useful.

Do some service for others, for your community or tribe while waiting. This will grease the wheels of the abundance train coming your way.

All aboard …

6. SONG DISPUTE/CONFLICT

䷅

Above	Qian/Gan	Heaven, energy, Spirit power
Below	Kan	precipice, water, danger

The wisdom

There are arguments brewing within.
There can be no completion.
Do not be afraid or intimidated.
Stand steady in your center.

Go easy on yourself, for this time is not meant for completion. During times of conflict, whether it be in intimate relationships, business, or the family or tribe, there is no way to see clearly what must be done to regain peace. The only place, therefore, is in the center, the place of inner balance. It is not weakness to take the center point where clarity resides; it is wise. By remaining neutral while others plead their case to the authorities or bully and coerce in order to be right, you will gain clarity.

In reviewing the situation you will likely see that when you entered into the present arrangement or agreement you were not clear or were in denial about the truth of the situation. Often we are blinded by unrealistic expectations fired by our desires. Go back to the beginning of the situation and root out where you missed or denied your truth. Do not let this reevaluation activate further conflict by trying to correct the situation. It is not correctable in its present form. If you try, it will bring further conflict, and any argumentation would blind you to the truth.

The hexagram Song advises you to withdraw from the situation long enough so that you can more clearly see what's happening or has happened. You may decide to withdraw completely, seeing that the agreement, whether actual or inferred, was based on false premises. If your choice is to proceed, the benefit is to recognize that conflict is being felt by all involved. With a firm stance and an open heart, meet the opposition halfway. Negotiate up to the point where you feel there is fairness and you have clarity of purpose. If no fair resolution is possible, then without further delay move on, no blame. Whether you stay in the situation or leave it, the clarity you gain through this process will bring you peace of mind, and that will pave the way for eventual good fortune.

> This conflict cannot be resolved
> By taking sides;
> Move to the center
> And observe both sides with equanimity.

At present, conflict is amplified in our world to an extreme. Everywhere people are at odds with one another, and political posturing based on power, place, and money is running rampant. Meanwhile, we have lost sight of the harm being done to our planet and other species. You are picking up on this collective negativity and fear; it can't be helped. Greed has caused people to fight to control nature. It's hard to wrap one's head around why they think this is even possible. Look to the tides, the weather, to anywhere where humans have challenged or tried to "tame" nature and bend her to their will. It's a ridiculous battle, one that can never be won, as nature will always prevail. It is the ego of humankind that must be tamed, not nature. It is the illusion of separation—from Spirit, from nature, from others—that must change to allow the flow of life and love to move us into harmony and balance, into a new way of thinking and being on this planet.

To bring about the success you desire, face your fears. Look to what is causing discord and deal with these issues first from within. To do this, disengage from the emotional state the conflict has activated in you. Then cultivate a clear picture of all sides of the situation. From this more balanced perspective you will see what must be done; you will be acting from your inner sense of fairness and truth, and not out of fear or trying to appease others.

In personal relationships, cultivate compassion and listen fully to your partner. In business, communicate with focus and empathy for your associates. Do not be afraid to speak from your heart. In this way you will be heard as you speak your truth. Look to where you are rigid and demanding of yourself or others—the one is usually connected to the other. Give yourself a break and adopt a point of view that takes the pressure off. Take an inventory of your goodness, skills, and intentions. In knowing that you are enough, you will make the right decision. It may be to withdraw from the situation completely, or it may be to begin anew, with a more flexible point of view, negotiating a place of fairness and harmony for all involved.

This reading is a teaching for what may be a situation at hand, or it may be a lesson in how to proceed in the correct way in a new situation that's just on the horizon. At the beginning of any enterprise, be it business, art, love, or any form of group endeavor, listen carefully to what the other says. Do not dismiss the subtle doubts and nagging sense of unease that you may feel in your communications. When beginning to get to know someone romantically, listen for clues as to how the other person has behaved in the past. Often they may say they are not good at relationships, or they are not ready for a relationship. Listen to this and go no further. In business or other group endeavors, investigate how others in the field perceive your colleagues. Listen to what they are saying about past deals, previous partners, or other involvements. If you sense negativity or dishonesty, do not proceed. Bow out gracefully, without judgment. If you're an artist, choose your representation carefully. Ask the hard questions, always knowing it is you they need, not the other way around.

If in the situation you do not know which way to go, it's a sign to disengage, to go to the center. From that place of balance you will have a clear picture of the situation in its entirety. Once you have gained this perspective you can act with confidence and grace. This will lead to a good outcome.

7. SHI THE COLLECTIVE

䷆

Above Kun — center of Earth; that on which everything rests; the basis of all things

Below Kan — gorge, precipice, snare; the taking of risks; the danger of swift-flowing waters

The wisdom

Power to the people!
Bring your legions together.
Alone you will only survive;
Move together and you will prosper.

What lies ahead in your situation is nothing less than great. It will require great risk to achieve even moderate gains. Not that your gains are restricted in any way; it is quite the opposite, in fact. The field is wide open, the potential greater than great. It's just that it requires taking a risk.

Implicit in this hexagram is the cosmological metaphor of being at war with all that has held you and the whole of humanity back from the physical, environmental, and spiritual leap of faith that is necessary and possible at this time of energetic shift on Earth. And she is in jeopardy. Shi says that to clear the way for yourself, your family, your tribe, and the collective, you can no longer be the ordinary civilian standing by, a mere observer of the rush of activities flooding through your personal reality. You must enter the fray by accepting the mantle of leadership in your personal journey and in the collective. We're talking basic social responsibility—your responsibility to the greater good.

The benefit is in carefully and thoroughly aligning your inner life with your movement forward. You can then martial your forces and set about readying to meet the challenge. There are some very real forces, both inner and outer, that are being triggered as a response to your quest for achieving progress and attaining contentment and peace of mind. You are the leader of your quest; do not look outside yourself for answers. As a leader you are called to service.

Be disciplined as you marshal your inner forces, your legions. The challenge, or test, before you must be met with an organized plan that is directed not by the ego, but from trusting your inner knowing. *Conjunctio* is a Jungian term to describe the union of opposites, as in the union of the conscious and the unconscious. This is what is called for now—the conjunctio of heart and mind. In this way you will not be harmed and will emerge victorious by meeting the coming challenges with integrity, compassion, and honesty.

As you neutralize or defeat the negative forces or influences, you will merge with the great flow, the cosmic flow. Then, as your abundance package unfolds, do not fall prey to the ego's background noise as it attempts to lure you into a victory lap down the red carpet amid the flashing and clicking of the imagined paparazzi. Be humble and use this energy to calm the mind and nourish the loving heart of the collective. Let your victory quietly benefit all, as all are in need of healing. Still your mind and stay in the flow that you have sacrificed so much for. Less in the way of display is needed at this juncture in the time wave.

Deconstruct your deepest fears. Be ruthless with yourself as you examine your penchant for drama. Bring truth to the lies you have told yourself about not being good enough or feeling inadequate to the task of leadership, concerned that if you face everything boldly, fearlessly, you will fail. In this you cannot fail; the nature of the quest is such that those who enter it with integrity and compassion cannot fail.

Once you have assumed the role and proper level of leadership and have taken the first step into risk consciousness, you will be nourished by the influence of awaiting abundance. All you need do is start, cross the line in the sand that is right in front of you, and there you are, right where you need to be. It is here that you will have the vision, strength, and confidence you need to accomplish the goals of this sacred journey, the role of being in support of Gaia and the New Earth community. The growth this will bring about will benefit your relationships, your tribe, your associates, all sentient beings. Most of all it will work on the inner planes to free you, to feed your spirit and bring you in touch with your divine self in the interconnected whole.

> You are gathering by the river to marshal your inner
> forces.
> Take the transformational leap into risk;
> Open your eyes and your heart and fear not;
> Risk is your companion, your energetic fuel,
> Not your enemy.

Now, as you face a karmic challenge, whether in a personal relationship, in business, in your health, or in your emotional or spiritual well-being, you are called on to gather all that you have learned to make a shift in your personal situation. In this way you will triumph and be one with your inner light and your powerful and well-honed inner forces. Spirit is recognizing you and your actions, and this pleases Spirit.

You are called to the collective, to roll with your helpers on this great adventure. Look to them and praise them. Point out their strengths and judge not their weaknesses—or your own. Consider that you have an army of companions, whether near or far, who will support you across the divide, the place where Spirit emerges and connects you with all. Trust the feeling of oneness, for it is in oneness that you will find you are not alone.

8. PI UNION

䷇

Above	K'an	water
Below	K'un	Earth

The wisdom

Our dreams and desires
Flowing together,
Finding union in the sea.
Ride the river.

The elements water and earth are united. Together they form a natural and beneficial union. Water needs no guidance as it begins its flow toward the sea; it finds its own way and seeks its own level. Your path now is similar in that you are drawn to harmonizing with others who match your energy and flow. These are the laws of attraction.

When you hear the sound of water flowing in natural settings, it brings a sense of peace and tranquility. There is a primal knowing that these waters are traveling to join with larger bodies of water. And in that joining, that union, great bodies of water are formed. Along the way, these waters nourish the Earth. Embrace the knowing that all are one with the waters and one with the Earth. This is a powerful message from Spirit. Consider your tribe, relationships, and associations as rivers that are meant to join together to carry you safely and joyfully to the great sea. The flow of this synergy will carry you to love, happiness, and accomplishment.

Union can bring happiness and form.
As waters join together they create new pathways.

When people are brought together
Through love, trust, and compassion
They create new pathways.

In this journey be cautious of promises that tell of advancement without work. Joining is work, the most glorious and beneficial work. Know that this is your path to a free mind, an open heart, and a satisfied soul.

In business, make stronger ties and cultivate the networks in your milieu. In relationships, be of pure heart and show and speak your truth. Be confident in reaching out and strengthening ties with family, loved ones, and your tribe of friends. If trust is lacking, create it through your transparency of feelings and knowing yourself. If you find that old patterns or connections are toxic, then offer them to the ritual fire, where they are reduced to their elements and can be remade into beneficial patterns that nurture you.

In this hexagram, Pi, the essential message is that the time is now to actively create positive change for the betterment of all and to nourish a new vision of Earth. When so much is available to you there's a temptation to act for personal gain and to neglect your connection to all beings. This lack of consciousness would cause your hard-earned upward spiral to descend. The negative aspects of ego will attempt to activate an uncalled-for greed to have more—more happiness, more money, more influence, more love, more … stuff. This is an aspect not only of our ego-driven, insatiably materialistic society, but of the human condition in general, and should thus not be judged—but do be on guard. Consider that you have all you need at this moment in time, and it will be recognized and made useful by expressing gratitude for the life that has been gifted to you. Your spirit dancers are with you and are ready to assist you. With an attitude of gratitude you will be clear about what you truly need and what or who is to be surrendered to the ritual fire.

If you find yourself feeling that you do not have enough currency—i.e., energy and life force—in your present situation, do not fall into the widely accepted definition of currency. You will find it is not the currency of money, influence, or power that is needed. At this time and in this situation it is compassion and goodwill. True, goodwill and compassion alone do not pay the bills. But when these qualities are combined with joining together with trusted comrades and community members, it can become the flow that will allow you to manifest contentment and abundance for yourself, your tribe, and your community. You will be led to your bliss.

Trust is called for now, trust in yourself and trust in those close to you who have proven their sincerity and goodwill. Pi speaks of the waters flowing over the Earth and joining together at seemingly random places to form lakes and oceans. But the flow is not at all random. You, like the waters, are being moved by an inner, primal flow of the precious material of the soul; your task is to simply allow. Get your ego out of the way, quiet the voice that says you must look good to others. If you let go and allow, you will find truth and flow. Trust that you will be taken to the sea of creativity, love, abundance, and contentment. This is called nurturing the soul.

Pi relates to the need to unite to accomplish change for the greater good as well as for the individual self. New relationships built on trust and goodwill can now be formed. They should be conceived and allowed to grow in an incubator of compassion, truth, and trust. This union will provide benefit in proper measure for all.

In the original text of the Yi Jing, the earliest form of the Book of Changes, there are subtle instructions on magic. Pi contains a powerful lesson on this subject: step out of your old mode of "me," be it self-pity, self-sacrifice, self-destruction, or self-aggrandizement, and consider your place in the whole. Through spiritual practice, inner work, prayer, and ritual, commit to releasing and shifting negative patterns. Trust the magical self within who can, with beauty and grace, strengthen your bonds to all those around you. Be a leader in your tribe, business, or community. Show compassion and support for your fellow travelers. In your personal relationships, do the same.

If you work with a group and do not feel the desire to lead, then joyously join with your community, tribe, friends, family, and associates to accomplish tasks for the greater good. Acting in this manner will lighten your heart and allow you to see clearly where this flow of energy, trust, and compassion will take you. In this space, fun is born. Wherever you go in the adventure before you, consciously spread loving light. Work to join people together. There you will find comfort, and your difficulties will be washed away, leaving the path clear for positive change to take place.

In the natural world, tiny brooks and streams join together to create rivers that flow into lakes and eventually to the ocean. It is like that for all of us at this time of shifting into a new paradigm. It will be evident when you allow your own ideas and those of your fellows to flow together to make something greater than individuals could imagine or accomplish alone. In this way the landscape of the New Earth will be seen and will serve as a goal, an ideal of what is meant to be, even through the lens of the difficult times we now face.

The antidote for worry and doubt is trust and compassion. Reach out with the strength of the warrior, the goddess, the hero, and radiate love and trust. Be love, and trust those who have shown you their purity of truth. These are magical teachings, and you, right now, are the magician.

You are the one you have been waiting for, no doubt about it.

9. XIAO CHU THE SMALL ACCUMULATING

Above Sun root, foundation, nourishing
Below Quin/Gan Heaven, energy, Spirit power

The wisdom You are entering a time of great potential.
Heaven awaits the lightning,
Lightning beckons thunder;
You are the thunder.

Progress has been good, yet completion is elusive. Giving in to frustration will take away your power, and the goal will slip further away. Be confident, and you will find that completion is not the benefit now; the real benefit is to focus on the present moment.

As you proceed on the road less traveled you inevitably come up against obstacles like guilt, shame, and judgment. These obstacles are showing at precisely the right time. Your inner strength, wrought through hard work and suffering, is at its zenith; it's like a finely honed sword. Raise the sword and cut away at the ties that bind you to old patterns and empty relationships, whether personal or professional. In this moment be the skilled warrior who knows that a sword this sharp is a sword with two edges: on one side it can cut through a lifetime of ill-fated patterns, while on the other side, if you do not come to battle with a pure and considered intent, it has the potential to slice away at your resolve and leave you powerless, unable to go any further.

At times like these, progress will be made by going inward rather than forward, paying attention to the small things. There are a number of tasks to be addressed at this juncture. Set grand ambitions aside for now and attend to the details, so that your path, your vision, will become clear. Clean up your desk, straighten the closet, clean out your car if you have one, balance your accounts, and lighten your load. Give some of your stuff away, literally and metaphorically. These seemingly small gestures announce to the universe that you are putting your house in order. As well, when it comes to relationships, projects, or health matters, deal with the particulars; vow to remain true to yourself and have honest, open communication with all those in your life. Act with minimal verbal flourishes; in this way you will have success in small measure. This is good enough for now—the power of the small, which is greater than great.

At this point you will then be able to dip into the subconscious and bring to light the negative beliefs that have been blocking you. Make the darkness useful as in stillness you go inward to cultivate self-awareness, which is found in the union of light and dark, yin and yang.

In life's journey we suppress our dark side, our shadow. In the deep recesses of the unconscious you will likely find some ugly old stuff: disappointment, guilt, betrayal, abandonment, and shame. It is in these dark, shadowy, troubling waters that our negative patterns and self-doubts arise. Mostly this shadow side is denied and projected onto others—partners, friends, associates. But if we dare to we can know our shadow, and therein lies our liberation from fear and the key to activating our full potential. Just remember that when engaging the shadow be aware that you are dancing with the dark side, and if your intent is not for the greater good, you will be derailed. Meet your dark side head-on, in the full light of love, acceptance, and compassion—for yourself and others—and it will dissolve. This will lead to a stronger, lighter you, a more sustainable you, a you who will love fully and able to receive the love and abundance you have long desired.

Look unabashedly at your dark side and don't allow shame or guilt to cause you to avert your gaze or shirk from the task. We all have a dark side, a shadow self. There are great gifts in these recesses of human consciousness. Don't be afraid—it is nowhere near as bad or as dangerous as your ego wants you to *think* it is.

The crux of this reading is in this traditional Native American prayer:

> Oh Great Spirit,
> May we cherish the gifts of Creator;
> May we hold the beauty of the world close to our hearts;
> May we embrace the spirit of peace on Earth;
> May there come to all people an abundance of Earth's greatest gifts:
> Health, happiness, and enduring friendships.

Use this prayer in contemplation of setting out each day. Prayers such as this open to the Tao, the way.

Being diligent about your meditation practice or developing one is of great importance now, because it is in stillness that you make a relationship with the Divine Feminine and thereby open to your full human potential. Every day give yourself some moments of quietude and inner spaciousness. In this vast place within yourself is a universe pregnant with possibilities, where you will once again fall in love with life and with your own true self. In this way you will feel the unity of all of we struggling beings, and you will touch the heart of compassion. Know that your guardian angels and guides have your back. You are safe. Just do the work. And know that we are each the New Earth.

10. LÜ MATING WITH THE TIGER

䷉

Above	Qian/Gan	Heaven, energy, Spirit power
Below	Dui	open, easy, responsive

The wisdom

It is coming your way.
Slow down so you can hear.
Between each step feel the pause;
In that pause life resides.

The desire to mate with the Divine must be well-timed and approached with an open heart and a quiet mind. Now, in pursuing the path of higher consciousness, you have been led to the tiger's cave. This is where one mates with the spirit tiger. This mating is an acceleration of your quest.

Your path to a higher state of being has often felt like a difficult trek up a steep mountainside. On this peregrination you have faced dangers, disappointments, and uncertainty. Yet even with these challenges you have made small, almost imperceptible advances. The benefit that Lü is describing is that your small accomplishments have led you to this pivotal point.

You have come to a place of honor where you are asked to make an offering at the altar of the Divine. If your offering is correct and your approach dignified and humble, you will be made whole and can mate with Spirit. If your approach is too fast, ill-considered, and without grace and compassion, and if you do not adhere to your tribe's tradition of good behavior and honor your fellow beings, the tiger in the cave will not be a holy, beneficent guide to higher consciousness; it will be a fierce guardian of Spirit who will chase you out of the cave, and you will roll down the mountain, back to the beginning of your journey.

This journey, though desired, spells danger. Not the danger of death—the danger of remaining in spiritual and emotional isolation.

You have come to a crossroads where you are asked to choose one of two paths. One is hidden in shadow. Beyond the shadow the path seems clear and even, promising abundance and satisfaction. The other path is steep and challenging; it promises nothing and contains no glimpse of success or conquest to entice you. This path is fraught with challenges, as it goes up an almost vertical mountainside, but it leads to a satisfied soul. There's something familiar about this difficult path. Perhaps you've chosen it before and have made progress, but this time much more is at stake. If you were to follow the easier path as your ego would prompt you to do, you may make it to your goal unscathed on the outside, and others may even praise and honor you, but on the inner plane Spirit will not allow you into the mating cave. So you would make certain gains but still feel empty and somehow unable to connect with Spirit force. The difficult path, on the other hand, leads to union and bliss.

Having companions on the journey into the tiger's cave is of utmost importance, for you cannot do this alone. Choose well. This is not the time to try to lift people up to your level, whether in business, social interactions, or in personal relationships. Be kind, loving, and compassionate to all, but be cautious as to who is rolling with you at this very important juncture on your journey. Giving your power away at this time would be disastrous. Fully embrace the power of *no.* Look to those who share your goal of working to benefit all.

Nurture kindred spirits with loving-kindness, fierce
honesty, and dignity.
Be a soulful companion to friends, associates, and lovers
who seek the greater good.
In this way you will find what you've been looking for.

It's important during this process of personal growth and in your desire for change for the greater good that you treat others who come into your life with loving-kindness, no matter what position or attitude they may hold. The way you are in the world is your soul's reflection. If your interactions with others are tinged with mean-spiritedness, disrespect, or harshness, that negativity will stick to your energy field; this energetic dark fog would be felt by all you interact with, be it family members, friends, associates, or strangers. This energy repels the good and attracts more of its own kind of negativity. In short, you will attract exactly what you project. This would blind to your true path.

In essence the oracle is saying that if you are not fully aware of your conduct and have your head lost in fantasy and greed, you will be part of the negativity that is eating away at the world's peoples. By being aware and showing kindness to all, you will be protected, supported, and loved. You will spread your light to all, and your actions will bring hope to others who are lost in darkness.

Simple good manners that we should have learned as children, as in the words *please, excuse me,* and *thank you,* carry a lot of weight as we move through our days, as does showing respect for all sentient beings, including nonhumans.

Look scrupulously at your inner conduct. If you find jealousy, greed, judgment, or harshness in your thoughts, you will be lifted by simply becoming aware of these mental projections. Correct them and let them go, no blame. The words you think are more powerful than the words you speak. When you hear your negative thoughts and change them in a brief moment of recognition, this action of awareness, as simple as it seems, will free you.

At this time good manners and proper conduct can open the door to love, health, and abundance. This kind of correct behavior will bring joy to you and those around you. Joy nourishes creativity. The joining of joy and creativity brings a deeply felt satisfaction that is a healing balm to heart and soul, opening the doorway to prosperity in all things.

If you love, speak of love; if you are grateful, speak words of gratitude; if you are in need, ask for assistance with grace and no expectations.

11. TAI — PEACEFUL PROSPERITY/HEAVEN ON EARTH

䷊

Above	Kun	center of Earth; that on which everything rests; the basis of all things
Below	Qian/Gan	Heaven; energy; Spirit power

The wisdom

Correct connections will be made.
It is the time.
Heaven and Earth are joining;
Intuition is your guiding light.

The influence of the dark forces is now fading. Conflicts can be resolved. This is an auspicious time, when there is harmony on Earth. Gratitude for this time will enliven this rarified air so that all can now breathe equally and together. Where there are conflicts or obstacles, approach them with no fear. Peaceful resolution is possible. Quiet the ego and move without judgment of self or others, and the road to peace and prosperity will open.

The message of Tai is to inform you that you have, through diligence, called on the laws of attraction. This message comes in two parts. First, note well that within reach is a never-before-accessed storehouse of love, abundance, and clarity. The projects and relationships that have stalled can now be activated. The second part of Tai's teaching is this: with access to these blessings comes the responsibility of the visionary to check your intentions and behavior. Remain humble and prepare to receive. Because of all that you have sacrificed along the way, you have made way for this energy flow, which will be powerful, and in some cases perhaps even jarring in its intensity.

> Friendships can be renewed,
> Long-drawn-out battles will be resolved;
> Through persistent small efforts
> Peace and harmony can be achieved.

Make ready your connection to Source in body and in consciousness. In this way what will come will have a proper container. There is no doubt these gifts will come, but without correct behavior and thoughts they will vanish like a morning mist above a lake. Savor times like these when all comes to order; wear them like a warm cloak on a winter day.

Your benefit is to be proactive, aware, and awake to accept this energy, to make connections, complete tasks, and discern who are your allies and who are your detractors. Embrace your allies, whether near or far, and dismiss the detractors. Ferret out the ones in your sphere whom you must constantly pull up to your level, and lovingly release them, be it a friend, associate, lover, or relative. You will find that flattering attention is without substance and will ultimately be draining and destructive.

You are entering a new time of connectivity that can open the channels for true and continuing abundance. This oncoming force, imbued with an open consciousness, can now neutralize any doubts you may have had about yourself and your life's work. You will now be able to ax the ego's voicings of doubt and fear that have woken you in the middle of the night and greeted you in the morning. They are dispelled.

This time of prospering has been activated by connecting to your inner wisdom, slowing things down and giving you time, through the tempering fire of adversity, to develop your intuition and strength of purpose. Now, as you call from within for guidance to bring forth clarity, you will be placed in the correct frequency, which will propel you toward the best and highest good—for yourself individually and for the greater, universal good.

Often we are advised or feel the need to go see the sage, the wise person in the tribe, the intermediary between you and the Divine. This is not such a time. This is the time to use and depend on your personal wisdom and intuitive powers, which you have been developing while being diligent on the path. With proper intention and by initiating creative ritual, your visions, plans, and desires will be made manifest and brought to life. Be mindful and crystal-clear as to what you want to manifest as this incredible surge of life force comes your way. Prepare body, mind, and spirit, and direct your intention toward the greater good. This will allow you to activate the magnificent, dignified, compassionate being you truly are.

> Choose well your target, and in stillness, focus.
> Point, aim, and move with skill and intention.
> Intuition is the archer's arrow;
> It knows the center of the target before it is released.

This is an auspicious time for creative projects and organizations that are working for the greater good. Sun Tzu says in in *The Art of War* that the great leader does not lead from the front or from the rear; the most effective leader leads from the center, the middle, where all is seen and all is possible. From this position it will be revealed who or what is not working for the good of a project or endeavor and can thus be removed from your sphere. This clarity will make way for guidance that has been waiting in the wings for you. Open your mind and heart to embrace correct thoughts and actions coming from your soul's depths. Honor those who have given you the strength to grow and create; this has been a gift of self-confidence, a confidence you will relish as the arrival of abundance in your career; love and health will also flourish.

Sexual energy, attraction, and sensuality are part and parcel of this oncoming tide of creativity. Spread this beautiful energetic manifestation of Shakti, the primordial creative energy of the Divine Feminine. Avoid the temptation to use this powerful energy to manipulate others to achieve your goals and dreams. To do so your goals would become diluted or would dissolve, and you would miss this time of completion and abundance.

The confidence necessary to take you to the heights you seek will come with knowing that you have shown strength of character and integrity through times of want, sacrifice, and obstruction. Your community and associates in your craft or commerce will now see you in this light of strength and self-assurance and will be supportive. Those who have judged you will fade into the woodwork. This does not mean that the forces that were impeding your progress in the past have vanished. They may have been made impotent, but they are still there, lurking in the shadows, fully capable of rising again should you fall out of integrity. So remain steadfast in your practice, meditation, or whatever it is that in stillness gives you strength and peace.

Set your intentions firmly and be a fierce warrior as you proceed in truth and dignity. From this position you will soon find yourself in a place of success and honor at the karmic table of abundance. Take only what you need and leave the rest for your fellow pilgrims.

12. PI DECLINE/STAGNATION

Above Qian/Gan Heaven, energy, Spirit power
Below Kun center of the Earth, responsiveness

The wisdom In times of discontent,
Self-sustenance and
Humility are advantageous.
You have no influence.

It is of utmost importance when consulting the I Ching that you do not look to the past, but rather remain fully in the present. This reading is not for what is coming, not for yesterday or even a few minutes ago. It applies to now. As the cycle unfolds, only the now exists.

On your chosen path toward accomplishing your goals you have encountered obstacles. This is in the natural order of things. The correct action is to stop. The advantage at this turn of the Great Wheel is to hold still and look only to yourself for wisdom, sustenance, and comfort.

Because obstruction has come on suddenly, you feel under attack, that you must confront what or who is blocking you. However, it is not the time to go to battle, but to move into sacred stillness. Look within for the sustenance needed to maintain your psychological, emotional, and spiritual equilibrium. This is an opportunity to move away from the noise and angst generated when reaching out for gain, place, understanding, and love. In introspection, re-creation can occur.

You have considered joining a certain milieu to make the road easier and not so lonely. Riches and honors are being mentioned as a further inducement; however, this is a trick of the ego. Should you join the group, you would be taken into their game—and a game it is, not a benefit or a path of honor. If you were able to ask them, "Why do you behave in such a manner?" the answer would shock you: "Because I can." And were you join them, even in cordiality, you would fail and fall from grace. Therefore, you are advised to follow in what you know to be the correct way of behaving and acting.

Know that obstacles such as the ones you have encountered are temporary and will soon fade. When you come out of retreat and make your move in correctness, you will find strength of purpose. Do nothing other than making this time of full stop useful. This period of stillness and retreat will allow you to access what you have learned and studied, what you have embraced and gained. It is all in you, waiting to be accessed.

Relationships and associations can change during this cycle. The benefit will be to refrain from conflicts, battles, or arguments, as there would be no beneficial outcome, and you could destroy what will, in the near future, create benefit.

As you make your way toward your personal goals there are times when you encounter dark souls, people with little humility or integrity; they are a reflection of your own shadow side. You know they are not of your own soul tribe, yet you guess that they could be useful. Be cautious about who you associate with. Limit your social intercourse to those you implicitly trust. If in this challenging time you try to engage outside of your trusted circle, you will be met with misunderstanding and discord, and you would be robbed of this opportunity to assert your integrity and rely on your own inner strength. Go into retreat mode with an open heart and chill.

> Look carefully at all offers that come your way.
> Do not act on them or accept them at face value.
> Contemplate all sides
> And wait, in stillness, for the truth to be revealed.

You are finding interference in trying to get things done or trying to get your mate, tribe, or associates to understand you. You can see it so clearly, why can't they see it too? Don't try to figure it out; the *why* doesn't matter—it's just that you are not heard. This is an opportunity for you to stop. If you refuse, you could bring danger, either on the physical plane or on an emotional level, where you have vulnerabilities. There is no person, book, cleanse, or process that will aide you at this point, so don't waste your precious energy running this way and that. When you are met with an obstacle, consider all aspects, both sides of the coin, and stop to contemplate. Being morally and ethically strong in times of obstruction will serve you well.

Do not fear the darkness of this part of the cycle. This darkness, which is in the natural order of things, will pass, and you will arrive at a clarity that will give you confidence and strength. Decisions you make and the actions you take when you move out of stillness will lead to a time of progress and fulfillment. Fulfillment is close, very close. But if you don't pull up on the reins now, you will cloud your vision and diminish the energy necessary to receive and embrace the gifts that are hidden. Walk into the mystery with no fear. Meanwhile, give yourself permission to play and dance the way you do when no one is watching.

13. TONG REN HARMONIZING PEOPLE

䷌

Above Qian energy of Heaven
Below Li radiance, the bringing of light

The wisdom

Have no fear and go to the altar.
Make an offering,
Gather your tribe.
The battle is near; you are unstoppable.

A multitude of situations and challenges have come into view in a cacophony of movement, thoughts, and deep-seated emotions. It is all happening in a great crescendo to reveal your truth to you. You will benefit from holding still and assessing each situation individually. The difficulty is that the elements comprising this flood of energy are interconnected. Some aspects will require down-and-out war, while love will salve others, and the remaining challenges will transform on their own if you get your ego out of the way in wanting something or someone to change. Trust your wisdom, not your knowledge. Clue: your heart is your compass; keep it wide open.

Gather your people, your fellow pilgrims, for you will not benefit from going this one alone, which would exhaust you. By gathering a force such as this, you will be unstoppable. This time of bringing the people together, working for a common goal for the greater good, is one of the most beneficial and exciting activities in human incarnation. It is primal, this calling on the forces of magic you have sensed, but until now have not fully tapped into. The energy you will wield is akin to a magical sword. This is as real as it gets. You have a mission, and it's in your face. As you have accepted the role of spiritual warrior and initiator, know that it comes with responsibilities—to yourself, to your tribe, and to the community. Be you a leader or a traveler, this turn of the page will alter you and the world around you all your days.

> Stand in your truth.
> Bring together the clan.
> You have manifested this time
> To benefit Gaia.

It is a time of creative transformation. Gather with your fellow pilgrims and share ideas that will ignite the flame of common purpose. This will imbue your family, tribe, commercial enterprise, and community—and indeed the world—with your vision. You are now without limits. The size of the collective doesn't matter—at this turn of life's wheel it's not about numbers; it's about truth and purity of intent. *Coherence* and *phase transition*—these terms from quantum physics describe how the paradigm will shift, one person at a time, to create a quantum effect.

Individually, focus on your purpose and craft, and appreciate how that feeds the whole. It is of utmost importance that each one of us finds the conditions that nurture the advance of the whole. Take a deep breath and find what you've been hiding or hiding *from,* and make a sacrifice at the ceremonial altar of truth, the truth of these times, the truth that is being revealed by gathering together with like-minded people. There is immense power in the collective, waiting for you to embody it and make it useful. It may be a geographic collective or one of shared purpose and beliefs that has nothing to do with a physical place.

The torch of truth you hold in your hand will illuminate what has previously been unspoken or hidden. Prepare a unified plan in order to proceed. You must have a solid plan. It may mean a total reorganization from the inside out, or it may mean dissolution of the old to make way for something new. Whichever it is, the truth will set you free. Make love or make (metaphorical) war, it doesn't matter which, as long as you move in concert with your fellows toward the common goal of benefitting all. Remember, I am you and you are me, and it's all a reflection in this holographic universe. Recognize and viscerally *feel* how we are one. Keep that in mind as you see you smack-dab in front of you—you leading and you following as you lead. The recognition of this esoteric principle is a great and awesome joy that will resonate through your entire being. This realization will allow you to open up and feel compassion for all who share this planet—especially those who we may be in conflict with. This is how we will survive these times and become something greater, much greater.

Be utterly honest with yourself and see the role you have played in getting to this dynamic turning point where you gather with the clan. Examine your old ways of thinking and acting, which will give way to new, honest, straightforward actions, be they in business, relationships, politics, art, or health. In every situation make dignity, kindness, and integrity your guiding principles. The synergy that will result from joining with the collective in this way will bring the whole group into coherence and carry you—and all of us—toward the highest and the noblest of goals.

Follow brilliant, heartfelt new ideas; work with others to bring them into reality. Use discipline and order to create structures, works of art, and ventures that serve all beings as we walk the road to enlightenment together.

14. DA YOU   POSSESSION IN GREAT MEASURE

Above Li — radiance, brightness, fire
Below Quin/Gan — Heaven, energy, Spirit power

The wisdom

You have great abundance;
More will come.
Dispel hatred and judgment;
Make way for destiny.

The message of this kua is symbolized by the trigrams for fire and Heaven. Fire, above, is strength, and Heaven, below, is clarity. This is a most auspicious combination. These elements stacked together indicate a time of abundance, improvement, and success.

Your efforts and good intentions have created abundance in many quarters of your life. By behaving well and prioritizing correctness, you are the guardian of your manifestations. Integrity and honor will bring even greater bounty. With this abundance comes greater responsibility—to your relationships, to your community, and to all sentient beings. Take council with those of influence, and in your gratitude for this time bring joy by sharing and shining this light that is in your care. Move away from negative influences. Dismiss detractors and honor your companions of destiny with hope and unconditional love.

The obstacles that once caused you to stumble are being removed, and obscuring clouds have parted, revealing a vast blue expanse. Remain in graceful reception. As exciting as this time is, do not become giddy. Remain calm. Your well-tempered passions will lead the way to gain of whatever it is that you have on your cosmic wish list. It may be wealth and recognition if that is well within the bounds of your soul journey and integrity, but don't stop there, for the outer is but a small part of the equation. You can now have clarity of purpose if you remain calm and refrain from indulging in pride, greed, and judgment. The call now is to look to your inner core, your true self, your Higher Self, as you consciously move into a time of stillness and contemplation.

> You are given a light
> To shine on what has decayed.
> It is your responsibility
> To restore what has been spoiled.

During the last cycle you may have felt like you were being teased by the light. At the very moment you thought you would grasp it, it slipped away—now you see it, now you don't, the joke of the cosmic magician. Never doubt that the universe has a wicked sense of humor. It opens your awareness and asks you to have a good laugh at yourself.

Through perseverance and your good intentions, great wealth, however you consider it, is now here and here to stay—provided you operate within the bounds of integrity. Be aware that Da You, while sounding the bell of abundance, also carries an admonition: that to maintain this joyous and abundant pathway you are instructed to refrain from arrogance, judgment, and self-delusion. Look to any lies you may have told yourself and lies you have allowed others to believe. Correct these thoughts and words, and with compassion for yourself, let them go. As you do this you will enter an atmosphere of innocence, which will melt away old patterns and family karma that has plagued you and your ancestors for many lifetimes.

Be without comparison to what others do or have; that is theirs and would never work for you. Honor yourself and the teachers and helpers who have crossed your path, and be sure to appreciate those who have sorely tested you as well, for our enemies are our greatest teachers.

Opportunity abounds now, in commerce, love, health, and spiritual and emotional development. Be generous in all things, and this time of abundance will continue to circulate through your life.

The ego tells us that with clever deception we can gain what we desire. This is the shadow self, the inner trickster, the coyote spirit. Do not let fears or doubts lead you to conclude that what is being presented to you is yet another manipulation by the ego to hold you in the bondage of feeling separate and alone. Look long and hard at your present situation and do not let the ego influence your actions and decisions. That would only prevent you from claiming the abundance and joy that is being placed squarely before you.

Trust and share the wealth and wisdom that now comes to you like a warm breeze wafting the fragrance of orange blossoms through an early summer night. That breeze is called *love,* and love is flow. Actively use love to illuminate your path and the path of those who walk with you. In this way your love, inner strength, and spirit will increase, and the harmonious circumstances that set things on their present course will be recognized and honored. To keep the current of love flowing in your life, be humble, move with grace, and exhibit good manners and generosity.

When well-positioned in times such as these there is a responsibility to family, associates, and your tribe of fellow travelers. As you feel more secure in your seat of abundance, give of your time and loving energy: to Earth's children, the four-legged, two-legged, winged, finned creatures, and to Gaia herself. Give recognition to the other nonhuman beings that cohabit Earth with us, the water spirits, tree spirits, spirits of the mountains. All on Earth are experiencing this leap of evolution, and at this time love will accelerate the process. There is transformative magic in cultivating this awareness, and you are the magician. In this way this blessed cycle will repeat again and again in your life.

Take this time and the joy and abundance that goes with it personally. It is yours. Sing, laugh, play, and allow yourself to love and be loved. Ain't nothin' to it but to do it.

15. QIAN HUMBLING

Above	Kun	center of the Earth; that on which everything rests; the basis of all things
Below	Gen	quiet mountain; unshakable, steady, firm, and still

The wisdom

You have begun to recognize your goodness
And it is good that you know it.
Now open to gratitude;
Be humble and modest.

You have so much right now—your riches in knowledge and spirit are the result of your constant striving for your inner truth. You can clear any obstacles and know your position in life by being humble. Possessing this vital knowledge and spiritual insight is an incredibly powerful combination.

Look to accomplishments in your career, your relationships, your heart, your spirituality. It is good to shine, and very necessary, so that your light illuminates the truth for your tribe to see. Know that you will shine much brighter in humility than you will in ego expression.

Quietly accept that you are of great influence at this time. The example for your circle is that of humility. This doesn't mean scraping and bowing. Those who make a display of humility are in essence exposing themselves. In this coming cycle, live modestly, without fanfare, serving others, all others. Great teachers dismiss any claims of their greatness and point only to the kindness of their teachers and the blessings of Creator.

Pull up on the reins;
No need to advance at this time.
Turn the outcome over to Spirit.
Your harvest is aging and curing.

The temptation as you begin to see the plentitude of the harvest is to begin to distribute it, using it to gain favor and more riches. This is a familiar song played by the ego to take you out of the present. Have trust that the river of abundance will find you; you have set the processes in motion, so let things be. This takes inner discipline and self-love. To achieve this state of being, find your stillness and journey into the emptiness that you experience when you close your eyes in meditation. That emptiness isn't empty; it holds all possibilities.

Make a subtle shift in the way you've been thinking. Not that your thinking has been wrong—just the opposite. You have thought—and maybe overthought—the positive aspects of obstacles, and you've handled most of these situations quite well. Consider recent losses of people or things that have made their exit or will do so soon. Don't fret; this frees you up for a new way of thinking and being. This is the way to remembering who you truly are, the real you that has been waiting to be recognized and brought forward.

When you find that lately the way you've been relating to others and doing things has brought satisfaction in some areas of your life, the tendency is to stick with these same methods. At this time, however, anything repeated soon becomes stale, especially during this time of dynamic change. Risk is the key now. Take the risk of letting go of the way you've gained what now is yours; be humble and moderate in your behavior.

Moderation in all things is the key to transforming the heart and mind, moving us toward the greater good. We are warriors and are called on at different times to be present for the greater good. Now is your time. Clear your mind and observe, letting go of any preconceived notions about how things should be. Why? Because you don't know, you really do not know. So to have the harvest serve you, you must make offerings to the higher powers, as this is what got you here in the first place. It is because of the guiding light of higher consciousness that you have any clarity at all.

You are being called to greatness, so first you must find your still point. Most of us need some form of meditation, however simple. This state can also be attained by aligning with nature and communing with the elementals. The precise technique for finding inner stillness isn't as important as the *intention* to remain inwardly still so that you can be receptive to the wisdom of your inner guides and teachers, your better angels.

Oftentimes when we attain success, old patterns try to reassert themselves, and before we realize it we're caught up in them. The knee-jerk fear that we might lose what we've recently gained, that something well-deserved might be taken away, or that we might be cheated causes us to behave without compassion and empathy for others. We become rigid with fear. We act as if our way is the only way and staunchly refuse to open up to other possibilities. If you're in business or in a relationship with someone who behaves this way, communication is hindered, and the feeling of not being heard can lead to emptiness and stagnation. If you're both acting this way, one of you had better wake up, and fast, as such a dynamic is untenable.

Exercising compassion and kindness in the face of chaos and the fear-mongers who come around us at this time is one of the greatest challenges, and precisely why we must seek inner stillness.

Walk with dignity, spine erect, so you will receive the full dose of energy being transmitted to and from Mother Earth at this time, entering through the soles of your feet and rising up through your chakras all the way to your crown chakra. What's going on now is unprecedented in human existence. Light is coming at us at warp speed. We are in a dynamic of rapid change here on Earth. Don't doubt it: outer sources, from other realms and universes, are assisting us if we choose to raise our collective consciousness. All you need do to assist in this process is be humble, achieve quietude, and let Earth's helpers and teachers transmit to you what is vital at this time. You can tap into it and feel healing coming through you, so that all you touch and all those you love will be enhanced simply by your humble presence. Get it? This is the lesson of Wu Wei: doing everything by doing no-thing—nothing at all except to be in integrity and humility, with compassion and kindness.

16. YU ENTHUSIASM

䷏

Above Chen thunder
Below K'un Earth

The wisdom

You are asleep.
Uh-oh
Thunder comes!
You are awake!
Oh yeah!

Thunder roars from the belly of the Earth, so deep and loud that it reverberates in your pelvis ... and in many ways it *is* at the pelvic floor, the root chakra, the source of vitality, physical strength, and the ability to act, adding force, vigor, energy, and warmth. It stimulates and excites, clearing blockages, sluggishness, and limitations. This kua signals the arrival of pure unadulterated excitement.

There are events that have just begun or are about to be placed before you that can either serve you or defeat you. There is a choice to be made: you can choose to use this time of enthusiasm to bring light and love to your family, tribe, your projects, and all those around you; or you can allow this great force to cause you to retreat and sink into that old, familiar apathy.

Don't buy into what has been programmed into the societal mind, that you are a lone particle out there in a vast universe that is beyond your influence. Your inner knowing will confirm that you are not alone—you have your tribe, your community of fellow pilgrims, whether they are within reaching distance or not. You have the reflection of you in the other, in all others. This realization of our inherent oneness is at the heart of the flow of universal energy; it is truth. The benefit is to fearlessly reach out and grab this truth. There is no judgment if you fail to do so, however, in that case you will repeat this pattern again and again until it is too late to get onboard this train of joy, abundance, and love that is waiting for you at the station. Be the shining light for your community and tribe. You are being watched. With no fear, take the risk of leading others, for it is in risk-taking that great advancement is made.

Be aware that a thunderclap, which is what this wakeup call is, lasts but a moment. This time of great arousal and enthusiasm will last only a wink in the larger scheme of things, so use it or lose it. But don't lose it! Joyfully grab that brass ring.

Gather your tribe around you.
Celebrate!
The time is now.
Balance enthusiasm with spirit.
You are renewed.

When the seasons change and thunder comes, it releases the tension that's been building up. This kua announces a metaphorical change of seasons, a change in your way of thinking and being. Use this primal force now at your disposal to incite enthusiasm in all those around you. Be the leader you truly are in your field of endeavor and in your primary relationships, tribe, and community. At the same time be humble in the face of this great force of joy and completion. The release of tension will cause tears and laughter to erupt simultaneously, a blessed release. You will feel your first chakra power of sex, light, and love.

Thunder over Earth suggests that an electrical energy that's been building up is now being released. So it is with you now. You have passed through a difficult period of time where you felt judged, and feared you were slipping out of favor. This is actually not the case; you are better placed than you might have thought. The crash of thunder is signaling a dynamic change, and you are being called to let those around you know that the time of change has arrived.

Like thunder, enthusiasm cannot be controlled, regulated, or held in reserve. Enthusiasm just is. Within the nature of enthusiasm are the gifts of inspiration and confidence. Operate in harmony with the Earth and allow this moment to activate your personal power and enhance your spiritual path.

Oftentimes people say they have no formal spiritual path but do have a belief in something that is difficult to pin down. This is where the teaching power of enthusiasm and arousal come into play—through celebration, a form of ritual, which is itself a spiritual act. Make recent events a reason to bring your fellows, your tribe, together, and lead them in celebration. Signify that you are alive by dancing to the rhythms of the Earth. This is what we all must do, and we must do it now, and not just for ourselves: Earth and all her sentient beings need our infectious enthusiasm *now*.

A window of opportunity has opened. Break the cycle of procrastination. Plan it, build it, honor it, and celebrate it. The *it,* of course, is you, and it is *us.* Celebrate your success, whether in art, business, love, or in your creation and support of family and community. Get off the couch and demonstrate your love for her, him, them, and all of us. Be the thunder that awakens the spirit of love and celebration in all those around you. Celebration is the path of least resistance. Use it! These are the immutable laws of the universe and the human condition. And in the end we are just that: delightfully and magically human.

It is in ways like these that we have an opportunity to make the world a better place—the world we have imagined and all want—as we strive for the greater good. We are on the brink of a new age, a new planetary era. In the name of love, will it to be so.

17. SUI FOLLOWING/ADAPTING

Above Dui — open, free, unhindered; an open mouth symbolizing quiet truth

Below Zhen — shake, excite, inspire; power comes from the center of the Earth

The wisdom

In following
Adapt;
In following be not blind,
But know you will be changed.

Sentient beings are seasonal creatures who change with the influence of weather and sunlight, emotions and passions, suffering and joy. Sui signals that you are now at a turning point, an inner change of seasons. You cannot speed up the sunrise or make slow the sunset. So it is with the great change that approaches now: it is inevitable.

Questions are to be asked of self at this turning point: Have you been following an idea coming from your inner voice? Are you being presented with a person or a new situation that has the potential to alter your life? Responding to these questions requires careful consideration and self-examination to reveal and trust your own truth, beyond any coercion by social pressures. This is the road less traveled, where you and you alone must prepare for decisions to be made at this most prescient moment.

As societal changes are taking place at a rapid rate, there will be presented to you an opportunity to follow an ideal, or you may be called to take on a role of leadership to facilitate change.

This change will have multiple faces, all occurring simultaneously, which can be confusing. You will see the face of change on the streets, and you will feel those changes within. When the call comes, it may be as an intuitive knowing telling you it is time to take action for the greater good. Consider carefully whether you will take a leadership role or choose to support someone who has accepted the mantle of leadership.

Whether you are considering following or leading, be certain that your reasoning is clear and your intentions correct. It would be a recipe for disaster if you pursued leadership based on gaining power or aggrandizement of the self. As well, be clear if you are tempted to follow a person or an ideal because of peer pressure or because it would make you look good to have that association on your resumé. A decision made in the light of the ego's grasping may bear fruit, but that fruit would soon rot. It's often that way within relationships, families, and groups where there is denial of the shadow side.

If you find yourself under attack or you are being influenced by negative people, move carefully within their tribe to gain a greater understanding of their point of view. In this way you will obtain what you need to know to adapt to the situation so that you can emerge unscathed.

> The Zen archer becomes the arrow;
> The arrow carries the intention of the archer to the target;
> Before the arrow is released
> It has already hit its mark.

The message of Sui notes that a calling is occurring, the call to follow a person or an idea, or an inner calling to follow the truth of what you know in your heart is right. In any case it is a calling to act for the greater good. It is time for change. You know it; you've been waiting for it.

This hexagram calls for hard work, and that is as it should be. But Sui also calls for balance, and what balances hard work is rest, ritual, and inner quietude. You must be rested and clear when you come to a turning point, whether in your career, relationships, commerce, or in your connection with the Divine. Take time to be good to yourself. Be still in order to hear guidance so that you may take your proper place. Nourish your days with meditation, music, and play, whatever helps you stay in balance. Make a practice of being a good friend, to yourself and to others.

Be kind and compassionate and strive to communicate with clarity so there is no doubt as to your intentions. Be humble and share the credit for the gains you will receive. In this way you will have a continuing flow of success and satisfaction.

18. GU DECAY/CORRUPTION/REPAIR

䷑

Above Gen — quiet mountain; unshakable, steady, firm, and still

Below Sun — root; standing on a firm platform to achieve a slow and nourishing penetration into the heart of the matter

The wisdom

You have the ability to greatly advance;
First look to where there are deficiencies in your life;
Take time to allow for correction;
Stay steadily on course and your advancements will be profound.

In your present situation there are areas of disharmony; they may be in health, business, love, or on your spiritual path. These challenges, however, actually represent a positive flow toward making an important course correction. Procrastination at this juncture is ill-advised; your truth lies in being practical and realistic.

You have been reacting to old ideas and painful experiences of the past. The benefit now is to examine these old patterns and make corrections. Reforming your way of perceiving things and adopting new, constructive ways of thinking will rectify any deficiencies that do not allow for the full flowering of your success and greatness. This requires the shedding of old skin. You will feel vulnerable during this transformation; your cloak of protection will be to remain mindful and in gratitude for this opportunity.

Examine the basis of your creations, associations, and relationships to see if you have been in denial that there has been decay eating away at what you have built and worked for. By conducting a diligent inventory of body, mind, and spirit, you will identify where and how the decay began. In finding the corruption at the foundation of your way of thinking, you can repair and renew. Your growth depends on this period of reevaluation. Come to stillness and make a concrete plan to correct what is in need of correcting.

In the original text of the Yi Jing the ideograms for this hexagram indicate you should "wait three days" before making any move to repair the decay, and wait another three days to allow this process to come to fruition. The reference to three days simply means a period of contemplation, meditation, and concentration. This is good advice, as the bizarre, unfamiliar aspects of what's going on now are not like any other time. Normally, when we spot something that's out of order, our first thought is to move immediately to fix it. In this situation, however, that would not be of benefit, as things are not normal. If you were to move too quickly you would gloss over the fine points that need attention and miss seeing the root of the corruption. It may be that an idea has been corrupted and led to an addiction, or it may be that a personal agreement woven into the fabric of your plan has been corrupted by greed or infatuation. Whatever the case, you are called on to move without fear into the heart of the matter.

> Three days before and three days after,
> Slow down and contemplate.
> This will bring liberation.
> Accessing your intuitive wisdom, you will know oneness
> with all.

It is imperative that you not jump too fast into this rooting-out process. Take your time. Look to what led you here. From this vantage point you will see clearly where you diverted from the path of truth and strayed from working for the greater good. As you undertake this period of contemplation, the benefit is an open heart, where your thoughts contain no judgment or blame, of self or others. This is the place of compassion. When you find an aspect of your situation that brings up fears, doubts, or shame, then you've hit on it—this is exactly where the present decay can be found. Go in for repair at this point. This may mean rooting out people or situations that are not in harmony with your truth. This is the action that will bring about change for the better and lead to progress.

A great and joyous transformation awaits you. Do not let what lies ahead during this period daunt you or cause you to stop because of fear of failure—or fear of success. As you contemplate, whenever negativity or doubts appear—and appear they will—recognize them, take a deep breath, and then, upon exhalation, let them go, using focused intent and prayerful listening to your intuitive voice of wisdom. In this way you will liberate negative emotions and send them into the light of conscious awareness. It's as simple as that. You may have to repeat this action until you feel the release, but it will work, guaranteed. And when you do this, you will be free to give and receive more love as you proceed on your path toward completion and accomplishment.

19. LIN NEARING/LETTING GO

Above	Kun	center of the Earth; the yin element supporting all things; responsiveness
Below	Dui	grow, harvest, pleasant, free, unhindered

The wisdom

The cycle of want
And waiting is ending.
A powerful time
Is on the wing.

In the recent past you hid behind a veil of nonrecognition, where your words, feelings, and ideas were not fully heard or were dismissed out of hand. You were not acknowledged for your gifts and good intentions and were not appreciated for your insights and creativity. It's been frustrating, to say the least, to have been locked down, misunderstood, and held in irons in a multitude of ways. Lin brings good news: the time of bondage is over. However, before you are fully released you will benefit from examining what you were hiding from and why you were in fear of embracing your galactic goodness and greatness. The result of this self-examination will be the ticket to ride into your fully stocked warehouse of the soul, where opportunities exist to move into what the sages of old identified as greatness.

This dip into the bath of spirit and love of life will awaken your kundalini, the life force of crystalline energy that rests in a sacred pool at the base of your spine, and from there flows into all the body's energy centers, enlivening your wholeness of being. This is the vital life force that connects each living being and all of humanity to Spirit, rising upward to be released as your soul takes you on one grand, glorious ride on the timewave of now, the bliss wave, the wave of exaltation.

In relationships, you have strived to be present, but appreciation from lovers, friends, and associates has been wanting. The effect has been that you have feared to show your best and highest good. You can now take a deep breath as the cosmic veil is lifted, and you will be seen for who you truly are. As you experience the reflection of your own greatness coming back at you from others, it will surprise even you, who have, because of intolerance and fear, held back your best stuff because you haven't felt safe.

Relationships are now set to bloom at their brightest and fullest as you release yourself and others from bondage. Socially, your arrival has been anticipated, and you will be greeted warmly. If you are in a political situation, your ideas and goals are heard and the votes are with you—have no fear of losing, for in this cycle you cannot lose. So choose your engagements and battles wisely and move toward your own and the greater good. This will be nurturing, enlightening, and most satisfying.

The I Ching speaks of and teaches only the now. The broad opening in life and in spirit that comes with this cycle will not last forever, so gather yourself, and if you are so inclined, gather with others of like mind and take advantage of this auspicious cycle, the grand season of growth on the inner plane as well as in commerce and creative endeavors. You are invited to come through this cosmic portal, where you can join with ancestors, guides, and sage teachers of oracular wisdom, philosophy, and love.

The veil of doubt and denial has lifted,
The ancestors are guiding you along the treacherous path;

Take comfort and have no fear;
You are not now nor have you ever been alone.

Note the emphasis on time and timing during these most significant of days. The energy shift on the planet is happening now and already exists in principle within all sentient beings. It is above as it is below. Do not doubt that you are ready to take this evolutionary leap. It would not have come were you not prepared. Your task is to remain calm and steady as the wave of transformation sweeps you up and takes you higher.

This cycle favors new or renewed partnerships and projects, and a new focus on health and inner growth. In all of it, foster your passion; it is passion that connects you to the primal, elemental force so necessary at this time. It is in your DNA and has been programmed to be activated *now*. This genetic trigger is part of the alchemical evolutionary process of human souls and will be influenced by the joyous dancing spirit that the ancestors have brought to you at this moment in time. Accept this gift and join in the dance lest you miss the opportunity of the ages.

We are witnessing the end of a long and very challenging cycle on Earth. The collective of souls is being shown the very beginnings of this long-awaited shift of the ages. You are invited to surf this wave of change and join with Gaia, of which we are each particulates, as she changes her vibration to be in harmony with the galactic order.

Consider that some people will make the choice *not* to join the shift and instead go on with business as usual. There is certainly a rather bland contentment there, but it will be found to be void of passion and depth of love. It is each person's choice. Know with clarity what *you* will choose:

Dignity
Integrity
Compassion
Kindness

Allow these words to influence all your associations, actions, and thoughts, for they speak of energies that are a highly regarded, long-treasured universal code. This code is the secret of the ages, one that will open you to being able to let go and be one with all—in unity, community, light, and love. Trust: this is the way it works

Avoid actions that muddy the road. Actively protect the solitude and privacy of those close to you. And never doubt that the cosmos is watching, loving, and laughing with you.

20. GUAN OVERSEEING/OBSERVING

Above Sun	root/tree/foundation; standing on a firm platform
Below Kun	center of Earth; responsiveness
The wisdom	You are now seen. You have exposed yourself And you cannot hide who you truly are.

You have been working hard to be on top of your game. Now the reality of your situation has set in. Examine where you have lied to yourself and diligently begin to correct your way of thinking so you can find comfort in being who you *truly* are. Even if you make a conscious decision to continue with a protective front, it won't work now. Safety can only be achieved through correct action, action in support of the greater good.

The time of the observer is being presented to you now. It is a window of opportunity. You can remain in the pain of grief, doubt, fear, and loss if you choose to, but in that choice you would repeat the same tired old patterns that caused this crisis of heart and spirit. You are the observer of the truth of who you are. The architecture of this hexagram denotes an observation tower. It is from this tower that you see, and from here you are seen. By observing, through stillness, the correct actions and the beneficial road to traverse will appear. From this vantage you will gain in confidence and perceive a life of harmony.

As the observer you cannot help but be observed. When you are seen, the negative inner voice of the coyote, the trickster, will try to convince you that you have been wrong in your actions, behavior, and thinking. This is where the lies about yourself are born. Change these thoughts and the trickster immediately loses its power and will not be able to take you off the path as has happened in the past.

Your ego would have you remain in a state of discontent because "it's the right thing to do." But by your diligence in quieting the ego's false voicings and changing your way of thinking, the benefits of this personal work will pay off in a very real way. You've had a get-out-of-jail-free card in your pocket all along, and in this case the name on the card is yours—*you* are in charge of your freedom, not the trickster who in the guise of righteousness tries to guilt-trip and shame you into giving up your place on the tower. There is no way around it: when you become the keen observer you will be exposed and seen. From here you will see what must be seen in order to proceed with the knowledge necessary to carry you further into your truth.

You have come to a time in your relationships, business, and inner journey where the benefit is to pause, find stillness in your practice, and listen. There are hidden messages awaiting you, messages that will take you toward fully understanding your purpose in your family, tribe, and the world around you. You must be still to receive. This is the pause between lightning and thunder and is precisely where you stand at this benevolent moment in time.

> With eyes wide open
> Contemplate your world.
> Your words are heard.
> Your ideas are met with acceptance.

What has been unseen is now revealed. The universal laws are at work, waiting to be known and put to use. You know how to do it—it's easy because it's the natural order of things.

From the lofty view of the observation tower you will see what you have not seen before. It will become obvious as to what must be done, who you will welcome into the trusted fold, who will be no longer be accepted, and what modes of behavior are appropriate. Root out all that is toxic around you. No matter how small the poison, if it is ignored, it will gain strength. Contemplate the apple with a small brown spot; if that small rot is ignored, the bushel is lost. This is your situation: you are the observer and must fiercely deal with what or who is poisoning the well. It may be a person or an old, convenient way of thinking where you have denied your truth. There is no doubt that now is the time to change your way of thinking, which has been based on beliefs that have caused discomfort and created obstacles on your path.

This is your time in the sun, the bright light that shows you your purpose and your place in community and tribe. Hold your head high and be a beacon of truth for your fellow pilgrims at this time.

As you clear the way, your voice is heard. Your creations are accepted, your eyes are washed clean, and you can see as never before the true colors of everything around you. Identify and trust the impressions shown to you in colors, shadows, and light. These are the symbols of your intuition. It is here you can enliven the seer within that has been at rest and not ready for exposure to the world. Unleash this power and trust what you see and hear. In this way your heart is renewed and you can love again. With fearless, spoken truth, the way will open for you to receive the love that has likely been patiently waiting for you. It's about choice, and the choice is now yours.

Know that as you follow your observations you will be safe and capable of dropping the fear that has obscured your true self. You will no longer need to seek abundance, it will find you; all you need do is let go and embrace the guidance that will come. It may come through your own intuition or through the words of a wise person in your tribe. It may be in a child's laughter or the song of the birds. Just pay attention … and listen.

As you sit on top of this metaphorical tower, be in active observation. You will only be able to see as much as you allow yourself to be seen, to be loved as much as you love, and receive as much as you give. Embrace the beauty of Gaia and your fellow beings. Music, laughter, love, and deep listening are your panacea as you walk the Medicine Path toward remembering who you truly are. And who you are is magnificent.

21. SHI HE — BITING THROUGH

Above Li — radiance; the power of consciousness
Below Zhen — shake; thunder rising from the depths of the Earth

The wisdom

Obstacles are no longer hidden
They are in front of you
Confronting everything you see as sacred.
Judgment and punishment are appropriate.

The ideas, processes, and behaviors that have previously brought you success on the path to love, peace of mind, and abundance are no longer valid; they've become obstacles. The small seeds of darkness that in the past you ignored and thought would go away have sprouted and now, like a pernicious weed, will overcome everything unless you take swift action and return to the light.

It seems that in many ways things were getting easier and you didn't have to work quite as hard as you did before, right? This, however, is the trick of the ego to take you off-center. Shi He comes now as a wake-up call. This kua uses the metaphor of an obstacle in the mouth that you must bite through. The time for action is now, while things are still ripe. The benefit is to examine each action, person, and process on your path, then make a judgment call. If the subject of your inquiry is working with you for the greater good, then it can remain; if not, eliminate it, or in some cases you will need to confront it head-on. When approached in this manner, with firmness, it will lose its strength and will no longer hold power over you. In this way you will bite through and eat the obstacle, the monster of doubt, shame, and fear. This is the way of the spiritual warrior.

When you resolutely examine the current situation you may discover that you are being blocked by a set of rules or beliefs that no longer apply to you. Root out the wrongdoer or the self-deception in your situation. It could be someone close to you or something inherent in a business arrangement or an agreement made in haste. Dig in and find it, and when you do, it will be necessary to use your strength of truth in words and actions if you are to make a course correction. There will be things that need to be said, and firm, even wrathful action may be necessary. This is the way to deal with this obstacle if you are to clear the way for a return to love, peace of mind, and abundance.

Be aware that being nice, kind, and compliant in the current situation is *not* what is called for. This is what His Holiness the Dalai Lama calls "idiot compassion," meaning actions that support an unhealthy situation. This is the time to unleash the wise compassion of the spiritual warrior, which says that some things are good and some things are bad, and one must choose to act on the basis of wisdom and genuine concern in order to avoid further suffering.

> To restore order
> You must bite through
> To the heart of the matter.
> If you avoid this action
> There will be no resolution.

Taking heroic action can mark the beginning of a new cycle for you. Yet before a new round can begin there must be an initiation, and there's no getting around this. You must confront the troubling situation before you in order to survive as a whole, loving, kind, conscious human being. So jump in. Your commitment in seeing this process through is about to be tested in an important rite of passage.

This hexagram, Shi Hi, is asking you to rigorously apply honesty and verity to the situation. If necessary you will need to chastise or reprimand those who have strayed from the truth in relation to you and your community and tribe, and dismiss them. In this way you will be relieved of the burden that is causing doubt, shame, and stress, and you will then be able to move forward toward a beneficial outcome.

Do not let the fear of being alone in the quest for truth keep you from taking action; take action! Eat the obstacle by confronting it one piece at a time. Your action will be supported by good omens that will appear to give you the strength and resolve needed to bite through, to open the doors of perception. *Break on through to the other side!* It's on the other side, the side that's not obscured by fear, greed, and control, that the truth resides. And it's by being true to yourself that your clarity will show you the way to your bliss and purpose. If you have been cheated, lied to, or used, it is proper that the person or the situation is made to face the consequences. This is done with strength and conviction, a form of wise compassion, and this is what's fair.

If somewhere in the back of your mind you're feeling edgy or have doubts, be diligent and seek the truth through a focused investigation. Seek counsel if you must; look behind the curtain that has been placed over the truth. Don't push away the uncomfortable feelings that your intuition is trying to bring to the forefront in order to signal you. You know the difference between right and wrong. This is the correct time to use your strength to discover and bring forth what has been hidden or unsaid.

You may be facing the possibility that your position in a personal, business, or social relationship could collapse and much will be lost. Don't let yourself be controlled by the fear of not being accepted by a group or by certain people whose opinion you thought mattered. Do what you must do to maintain your dignity and the highest standards of integrity. Reformation is in order, and you must do what must be done.

It may well be that there is something going on that is unseen or that has purposely been concealed from you. It may be something illegal or divisive; someone may be covering up an action done in the shadows or may be projecting a drama from their dark side onto you. Go within. Sit quietly in stillness and ask for guidance on how to proceed. With proper intent, all will be resolved and your strength will rise up when you operate for your own and the greater good. At that point fear will no longer have a hold on you.

By biting through what is untrue or unfair, standing strong for integrity and correctness, you will enter into a blessed union with the forces of compassion and love, the energetic of the New Earth, where we are all one, living in cosmic harmony on this small, beautiful rock floating in space.

22. BI ADORNING/REFINING

Above	Gen	bound, quiet, mountain
Below	Li	radiance, brightness, fire

The wisdom

Behold
A stunning moment is here.
Live to your highest standards;
Refine the outer aspects of your life;
Thus you will be blessed.

In life come moments of clarity. This vision is only offered, not commanded. Your choice is to live in a state of grace or continue in normality. Whatever your decision, no blame. Fear can be an awesome obstacle when a time like this is on offer. You will make great advancement and find your truth if you discharge your fear and deconstruct your doubts.

Do not attempt to press forward in your situation or affairs—not yet. Go into stillness as you quietly let your influence be noticed. You have not come to this moment of grace to put form to your future or to enhance the value of your efforts. And fear will only make you invisible. The choice now is to be seen—seen as you walk with dignity and grace. By refining and honing your outer form and social presentation, success and peace of mind will be yours.

This state of grace is the appropriate time for seeing, activating, and embracing the highest good—for yourself, your community, and your tribe. This is a high-water mark, one hard to achieve and maintain, so make no great decisions or commitments from this lofty perspective. Simply see with this momentarily enhanced view, and let things take their own form and fall their own way. Set small goals as you look to the details of your place on Earth. You have nothing to do other than to refine your original beauty and be the quiet witness and compassionate observer.

> Observe and honor the stillness you see in nature;
> Make these your symbols of change.
> Shouting from the mountain does not bring change.
> In humility you will receive.

Stillness might be considered a small thing, yet in its smallness it is great. As we tread the road less traveled, the path of the seeker, consider the importance of proper behavior. Good manners, ones that consider your fellow humans and Earth herself, set the tone for how the world as a whole will be and how you will be in it. In this place of grace what is yours will come to you, and there will be peace and harmony.

We are in an era of great change. Our survival—literal survival—depends on changing our ways of thinking and seeing. You can be the antidote to greed and violence by acting with impeccable manners and showing compassion in the way you treat others and how you behave in relation to your fellow brothers and sisters, to nonhuman Earth beings, and to Gaia herself. This is correct behavior, behavior that helps create harmony in the world. It is only in living harmoniously that we all can live in peace. It is that simple. The greatest advancement usually comes from the most elementary things, which are always available to you as you hone the fineness of your life.

The benefit will come as you use moments of clarity that are being offered to you now to adjust your attitude and behavior and correct any mistaken thinking. Do not take this time of momentary grace lightly; change is in the wind, and change is required.

Embrace the truth of oneness as never before—no boundaries of states or countries, species or gender. We are at a very delicate point: if we do not accept that we are all indeed members of one great tribe that need one another and feel one another, we are destined to experience more war, hunger, crime, greed, poverty, and the very real possibility of annihilation. All now have an opportunity to see the truth of the unity of all beings, and in so doing, to act with grace, good manners, kindness, and compassion. Reflect this to the world in all your relationships.

In the coming days, take some moments of quietude. Look to simplifying your life. Polish your ways in the world and make your adornments simple. Any issues that come your way can be solved in simplicity. It is now your choice; choose love.

23. PO SPLITTING APART

Above Ken mountain
Below K'un Earth

The wisdom
The laws of nature are incontrovertible;
Observe.
The Earth is shifting below our feet;
Stay in balance.

The Earth, by her contractions and expansions, her breathing, creates mountains. In this hexagram, yang Earth is pushing upward, causing yin to rise in the form of a mountain. This is an act of creation. For this process to take place, that which lies peacefully on the Earth must change as the mountain pushes upward. There is nothing to do but to accept this process.

Something you have built or cherished seems to not be adhering to the timeframe you had for it or is splitting apart. It's not that the project, situation, or relationship should be abandoned; rather, it's that you should keep still and take no outward action as the current change unfolds.

The hexagram Po is teaching us a lesson in letting go. It may be a career path, a relationship, some project you have been working on, or some aspect of your inner journey. It may be something you've cared for, praying that it would come to fruition. In letting go of attachments to outcomes, recognizing them for what they are, you can create a new path or direction.

You now have a choice: you can turn tail and run away from the issues facing you, in which case everything would collapse, leaving you with nothing; or you can observe this natural process unfolding and remain inwardly still while letting go of your old ways of thinking, your old attitudes and sense of entitlement, so that you can create a new, positive direction that will support progress toward your goal. The right action here is to not abandon your goal; it is rather to recognize your prejudices and judgments and then let them go. Simply put, relax the mind.

When you look honestly into the very heart of your present situation you will most likely find that you have been influenced by doubts and fears. These are obstacles. By keeping still, enhancing your spiritual life through meditation and by cultivating loving-kindness, you will find the spaciousness that further down the road will allow you to fully engage on a new, fresh level. In this way you will develop a new perspective that will allow you to realize completion—in whatever form that takes.

> The mountain rests on the Earth;
> Its foundation is broad and strong.
> The old is falling away,
> Leaving you with strength and a new resolve.

In everything there are cycles: increase and decrease, birth and death, fullness and emptiness. In your current situation it is now time to embrace the idea that everything that has been created, no matter how strong, contains the seeds of disintegration and death. This is natural. Therefore, now is not the time for heroic action; it's a time to be introspective. Allow the natural process to unfold in its own sweet time.

Letting go of old, hardwired patterns is truly one of the hardest things we as human beings can undertake. We become attached or even addicted to a certain way of thinking and being that we've applied to situations or relationships our whole life. The greatest potential is always present in any situation, but it can only come to fruition if we are brave and confident enough to be open to new ways of thinking and being, which can only happen when we relax into the flow of what is. This is the Tao, the natural order of the universe.

Po tells us that it's time to make a new blueprint for the situation at hand. Once the old ways of thinking and reacting are released, you will be ready to take that new, fresh approach. It is only by doing so that you will find your true path.

When a fire rages through the forest, it destroys most everything in its path, but it also unleashes seeds that will grow only after everything else has been consumed and destroyed. So it is in every act of letting go: there is a seed that will grow and become something wonderful and surprising.

It is not timidity to be in contemplation and do nothing; in fact, it is an act of great strength and wisdom. Practice being still; in that stillness look at your old patterns, thoughts, and behavior. Be the mountain. Feel your solidity on the Earth. From this vantage you will draw great strength. Trust that through stillness the correct way will be revealed.

24. FU RETURNING

Above	K'un	Earth
Below	Chen	thunder

The wisdom

It has been a narrow passageway;
All is opening;
Spirit hails love,
A joyous returning.

When a wound becomes infected it will not heal unless the poison is removed. This is your condition now. You have been in battle, and now you are returning, a bit battered and deeply tired, but you are returning, mostly intact. It is your ego that has taken the hit. The ego would have you think your retreat is somehow shameful. Don't go for it. There is no shame and no blame; you are human, after all, and this is part of the journey to wholeness and light.

On this return it is simplicity that will salve your wounds and heal your spirit. Old relationships too are being made ready to be healed as you come back to Source, the primal mind, made free of a troubled ego.

> The tide has changed.
> It has washed away what you built and cared for,
> Only to return and bring back what you thought was lost.
> Celebrate in humility and grace.

The great forces of Gaia can one minute blow winds that devastate the landscape and feed fires that blacken the Earth; then comes stillness, wherein there is the miraculous return of life. These are of the universal laws of nature, of life and death, leaving and returning. You now stand at the point of the freshness of return while behind you lie old, useless patterns of behavior and convoluted associations that have been fraught with difficulties.

Thinking and analyzing will not make summer return during the winter. One must simply trust the energy of returning. So it is with your situation now. Don't think it through. This is not the time to analyze; you've done that, and you're exhausted from it. Give yourself, and those around you, a break.

This is a time to return to clarity of thought and vision as well as to return to innocence, a time when what is now returned to your field of energy will inspire creativity and confidence.

Surrender. Let this cycle of gradual progress toward the subject of your inquiry happen with no thinking. Know that the coming tide moving you inevitably forward is unstoppable. Let it happen. Allow yourself to ride this wave to the shore, arriving refreshed and rested, not tired and weak from struggle. The needed rebirth will be realized not by pushing forward through the thicket of old patterns and promises. The energy will be found by returning, by following the breadcrumbs you left on the path so you could find your way back home. You sensed this time would come, and it has. And when you get here it will feel familiar, like remembering some lines from a poem you read or was read to you as a child. It is in that light of innocence where you will find the power of the creative and the strength to bring to completion and welcome that which you most desire.

Don't be surprised if you find members of your tribe coming your way to fill the gap of aloneness that you've been feeling. They couldn't find you before because you were behind a wall of self-involvement and self-judgment that obscured your true self.

Open your heart and mind to returning souls and beloved ideals; talk story; let yourself be loved. You have been so damn good at giving and fixing—now is the time to listen and receive.

Your mind has been so busy you haven't been able to hear or see which way to turn, where to seek the knowledge necessary to extricate yourself from the hold the ego has had on you. Now in this returning you are being shown promising paths to where self-knowledge is found, and it is this self-knowledge that holds the key to your freedom—freedom to love and be loved, speak and be heard, and the gift of coming to stillness where you can listen, fully listen, to the coded sounds of nature. And speak to you she will, through the perfume of nature, the calling birdsong, the flowing waters, in harmony with the beating of your loving heart.

25. WU WANG DISENTANGLING

䷘

Above	Ch'ien	Heaven
Below	Chen	thunder

The wisdom

Disturbance coming from outside your influence.
Be diligent and disentangle yourself.
Demonic forces feed on ignorance;
Become informed and act swiftly.

Look into all your associations and see where you have given your power over to others or have compromised when the benefit would have been to stand firm. This is a partial cause of the current disturbance in focus, form, or intention.

Metaphorically and in some cases literally you have had difficulty finding a comfortable place or way to sit, stand, or sleep. Fidgeting in place for so long has become tiring. Your thought processes and actions have been clouded by your desire for a successful outcome. This is futurizing, which has led to overthinking your situation and not living in the present.

By focusing solely on correctness, fame, position, recognition—outcomes of any sort—you are missing the point. It's not that you can't have these things—you can, and with attention to moving with and for the greater good, you will. What's problematic is your ego's projection into the future, which prevents you from tapping into your intuition. The call now is to be spontaneous and move with absolute confidence in who you are and what you want. The beneficial action is to disentangle yourself from any ties that have bound you to past influences and outmoded ways of thinking and acting, or reacting.

The trickster ego would have you look into the future and see the grand and shiny things that represent success, and the smartest, cleverest, coolest ways to move toward your goal, come hell or high water. But this arrogance would lead to a disastrous outcome, guaranteed. If you were to move in this manner you would be disregarding the influence of your spirit helpers, who bring the strength of innocence and inspire creativity. And you never want to lose that part of you that is the child of innocence; at this time it will be your saving grace.

> Consider the ignored part of your being,
> Your inner, sweet child of innocence.
> Slow down;
> Do not act out of fear,
> Else you will scare yourself silly.

Fear would have you looking to the future and trying to plan for every contingency. This would only sap your energy and ultimately prevent you from receiving your just desserts, which in this case are love, abundance, and happiness. It is wise to plan and be thoughtful, but limit your thoughts and plans to the present. In doing so you will make the journey truthful, peaceful, efficient, and more joyful.

Your balance along the path is to be of service to others and to Gaia, including the oceans, deserts, mountains, plains, and all of Earth's sentient beings. As you slow down and allow the inner innocent child to appreciate the beauty all around you, your strength will emerge. It will be a strength wrought not from pain or angst, but from peace, laughter, and joy. By admitting rest and fun in proper measure in your life, you will keep a clear mind that will be ready to handle the good, the bad, and the ugly with equanimity and poise. So embrace the moment; the magic is in the moment.

In literal translations of the I Ching this hexagram is described as "being free of forethought and reflection." This is good to remember, as it will keep you in the present, the place of innocence. Look neither to the past nor to the future: *Be Here Now.*

26. DA CHU GREAT ACCUMULATION

䷙

Above	Gen	mountain/sunset
Below	Tian	sky/Heaven

The wisdom

Intensify your focus;
Receive the energy and light
That has been seeded
In your heart,
Which will feed your soul.

The benefit now comes from achieving stillness, setting all distractions aside to open to your truth. Deconstruct the adversities on your path at the very moment of this reading. See them for what they are, and do not become entangled. This action will reveal that in essence you have done well these days in moving toward your goals. While others around you have been foolish and wild, you have, for the most part, remained steady and awake. Yet with all this work you have somehow lost focus and there is disarray. Achievement can be yours by being scrupulous with yourself and stripping away the lies of convenience.

You are now face-to-face with the core of your strengths, beliefs, and resolve. Plumb your depths to be certain that you have laid a strong foundation of truth and integrity, right action and clear communication. See how your current mental state has caused your belief in yourself to wobble. Fortify by reevaluating the correctness of your path and renewing your commitment to the greater good.

Now plant your feet firmly on the Earth and open your heart to your joyous dancing spirit, the free spirit that in the past brought criticism and doubt. Open to your dancing spirit in any way that suits you—it's no one's business but your own. No need to share your inner journey, this is your private storehouse of magic. In your own way, open to the grand force that surrounds you at this time and let it flourish deep within the private place where you go to contemplate, lick your wounds, and heal.

The mountain above in this hexagram indicates that you must hold firm and keep still; Heaven below indicates there is a treasure concealed within. Da Chu carries a threefold meaning: First, you are asked to hold your position, the mountain, as you approach the impending important and precarious situation that will be or is now presented to you. Next, you must be confident of your influence, and at the same time, with humility, look to the wisdom of the past—your own past and that contained in the history of your tribe and culture. Lastly, you are asked to combine the wisdom and the energy you will gain through proper use your creative force to cut through the falsities and illusions cast before you, which for convenience' sake you believed and took to heart. Dismiss them. No blame.

> Your creative force has been building;
> It is flowering in your heart and mind;
> It is now ready to blossom;
> Get out of the way;
> Allow Spirit to bring you home.

You have been diligently acquiring knowledge and wisdom on your journey. You've listened to the teachings, read the books, done the workshops, gone to therapy (or at least considered it), and now is the time to bring it all together in an alchemical elixir that will give you the strength and confidence to make your move. By synthesizing your wisdom and knowledge, you will be free.

It is a great and wondrous time that lies ahead for each of us, and for all of us united, and your creative force is being called to the forefront. And as happens with all gains, on our way we are met with challenges. It may be a project, a relationship, a spiritual undertaking, or some situation that is confronting you at this time. Whatever it is, know that you are on the approach to doing something grander than you have ever done before. The instruction of this hexagram is to find your stillness. By achieving stillness and harmonizing body, mind, and spirit, you will be amply prepared to meet the challenge, and in that meeting you will know that correct action is always for the greater good.

Now is the time, in stillness, to generate love by first loving yourself without judgment, blame, or shame. Love is a power that lies dormant within all of us, waiting to be released. Love is the contradiction to all the messengers of fear and those second-guessers and naysayers who cause the glory of the heart to wilt. Love and only love illuminates the collective will to good. Giving and receiving love in equal measure will bring you into harmony and oneness and serves Spirit and Gaia. This is what it means to work for the greater good.

Be generous with what you will now accumulate in spirit. Share your bounty with family, friends, and fellow pilgrims. Let benevolence echo throughout the world through your service to others. Share your vision of a New Earth. Eschew mindless acts that pretend to soothe the soul when in reality all they do is numb the spirit and disempower your emotional body. Cast aside all fears and be a witness to your vision of a fair and just world for all. It is in witnessing that Spirit hears you and will nurture you.

Look to your teachers and mentors; relearn their teachings. If you have none, then look to the loving beings of times past or to the higher realms. Take them as your mentors in life, love, and integrity.

It's true that sometimes there are fellow travelers who are stuck in the ego and hard to be around. Have compassion for them, for they are actually divine messengers, here to show you where your own ego is entangled and what patterns you need to release.

You have asked, hoped, and prayed for what is now at your doorstep. Now be prepared to accept it all with gratitude, humility, and an open heart. Without these virtues this raw power would not only be useless, it would be very dangerous.

Hold steady as this giant wave approaches. As you surf this awesome wave, feel its power in your body and heart. Use the energy now available to you for the greater good, and you will manifest your heart's desires.

27. YI NOURISHMENT/TIGER'S MOUTH

䷚

Above Gen — quiet mountain; unshakable, steady, firm and still

Below Zhen — shake, arouse, thunder, inspiration; receiving power from the center of the Earth

The wisdom

The ritual table is set;
You are both guest and host;
Nourish yourself and all those around you;
Partake in the alchemy of living well.

The architecture of this hexagram is an open mouth. It is symbolic of the hunger for knowledge of the self and the soul.

The call at this moment is to open to Spirit consciousness, the amorphous, unseen component of the soul. As you consider what metaphorically goes into your open mouth, be equally aware of what goes *out* of it. The words you think and the words you speak have great power at this time. What you are receiving and giving is love. The giving of love through thoughts, words, and actions is necessary if you are to partake of the divine meal, where happiness and peace of mind are served; and it is in unconditional giving that you are guaranteed to receive.

You have not been heard. So be it. By sitting quietly at the ritual table and sharing the initiatory meal with others, when you do speak what you say *will* be heard and will be what sets the tone on your quest for understanding, enlightenment, abundance, and love.

It is a time of creative transformation.
Transform your thoughts, words, and actions,
Be of service in the transformation of others who walk beside you.
Recognize your tribal brothers and sisters and keep them close.

At this time embrace the idea of being part of a great, cosmic whole, for these are tribal times, the gathering of the clans. There is a primal knowing that is being revealed and released as we join with our companions of destiny, be they near or far, as physical distance has no bearing on tribal associations in the emerging New Earth paradigm.

Your longing can no longer be ignored. Identify, honor, and dissect your feelings of hunger. If you refuse to do so you could lose access to the spiritual nourishment, the ritual meal that is before you now. Ask what it is you are longing for. What is this hunger that keeps you from focusing on and completing tasks both great and small, that creates that uneasy feeling in your heart and gut? The answer will not come from outside yourself in the form of a sage, priest, shaman, or wise person. It can only come from you, and will require perseverance and deep, pointed contemplation as to how you have been thinking and what spin you are putting on things to make your present actions and decisions feel like they're right or "enough." Don't be fooled at this point; it's not the time to take the easy way; it's the time of bravely moving into the depths to uncover the lies you've been telling yourself for years, the lies you've believed and that your ancestors believed for many generations.

With diligence and commitment you have already brought much to the table—for yourself, your family, and your community and tribe. This is good; it is proper to grace your fellow pilgrims with your bounty. You too should partake of what is beneficial. But do not become enraptured by the table you have prepared and linger too long in self-congratulation. This can be known by no other name than pride. Pride, as presented by the ego, would stop you in your tracks. Instead, consume only what you need at the ritual table, then quietly leave, for your journey has just begun.

When an initiatory process such as this one comes toward you, you will be teased by the ego, which will present situations or persons that look too good to be true. Don't fool yourself and become clouded by desires of the senses just because what's coming toward you now looks so good or seems so perfect. This is a familiar old trick of the ego, which uses temptation to have you fail this initiation.

The time of nourishment is necessary in this global initiatory process in which we all are active participants. As great societal changes are spreading across the world at this time it is incumbent on all of us to bring the awareness of working for the greater good into our daily lives. By acting with dignity, integrity, compassion, and kindness, and rejecting the shadowy negativity that will surely be placed on your path as a test of your commitment to the light, you will hear your inner voice of wisdom, your intuition, which will keep you on track. This voice will be your guide. This is the teaching of Yi.

Remember and believe that you are here for a reason, in the right place at the right time.

28. DA GUO THE GREAT EXCEEDING

䷛

Above Dui open, easy, responsive
Below Sun root, foundation, nourishing

The wisdom

The situation is great,
The opportunities are great,
The danger is great.
Stay awake:
You will receive in
Great and proper measure.

Offers, opportunities, assignments, responsibilities, and desires are rolling toward you these days. The I Ching points to the timber that supports the entire structure of the home. In this case, the home is you. The ridgepole of your structure is sagging from the weight. Immediately go to the place of sacrifice where unnecessary weight is deposited to lighten your psychic load. At the ritual altar let go of any successes or failures of the past that might influence your decisions moving forward. Avoid trying to predict the future. Come to stillness so you may know your capacity for greatness in your projects, in your relationships, in your community. Have no doubts, this is the time of Great Exceeding.

In the past one would say you are at a crossroads where you can choose one path or the other. That luxury is no longer available. Your benefit at this time is to walk between these roads, taking with you only what is necessary and in harmony with the essence of who you are at this moment in time.

You are now experiencing what is called the in-between, sandwiched between ideas and realities. The task at hand is to clear the decks, secure your load, and delve deeply into the meaning of relationships with others, your connection to Gaia, and your commitment to the greater good, for yourself and all others. This is a place of virtue and nobility, where love and true abundance reside. It can be yours for the asking. But before you ask, be sure that you are prepared to support and nourish what is meant to be yours. Look to see if your connection to Spirit has been clouded by doubting your worthiness or by lies you have been telling yourself and others.

On this road less traveled the voice of the critical ego will have a go at you to attempt to take you away from your truth and your connection to oneness. This ego voice may be broadcasting its messages through your inner life, health, work, and relationships. The ego's tool, the ever-busy mind, will use everything in its arsenal—shame, judgment, impatience, fear—to seize control. However, your desire for success, love, peace, and happiness, no matter how you define it and in what measure, is not to be feared, for when you are in integrity you have nothing to be ashamed of. This is a momentous time, in which the benefit is to act swiftly and decisively to cut the monotonous drone of the committee of limited faith gathered in the boardroom, the yapping ego.

Consider the importance of having a daily practice. From a place of mindfulness and stillness you will be able to see the source of the internal chatter that's causing turmoil and imbalance at this weighty time. Without regularly renewing stillness you will be in danger of becoming blind to correct behavior on your journey, as the mind will have its way with you. The energy of the Great Exceeding is here, therefore it is now time to leave the outcome, whether correction or collapse, to Spirit, and go within.

The action suggested by this hexagram involves looking into the heart of the matter to see the truth that resides there. This is an exploration led by the heart in concert with a still mind. Once you have done this work you may find that you are able to correct, and with grace, enhance the finer aspects of your situation. On this inner exploration you may find that a situation is damaged beyond repair. If this is the case, move on with no blame, guilt, or shame. You will then be free to move with an understanding of the lesson given by Da Guo.

> Do not try to salve your ego;
> Your action in the situation at hand
> Must be accomplished with mindfulness
> And a gentle hand;
> Any other way misses the point.

This time is well-represented by the Hermit card in the tarot, which signifies that there is a guiding light on your path, but you are walking it alone. It is time to be solitary, to meditate, organize, and find the truth in your heart. During this time of solitude, feelings of agitation or frustration will no doubt arise. No worries, no blame: these feelings will pass as you deconstruct them and shift the fear to love. Clarity, understanding, and enlightenment await you on the journey; give your mind a break and relax into this in-between state. The Great Exceeding calls on you to give attention to the now. Take a deep breath right now and nourish your body, mind, and spirit with your life force.

What is happening now for each of us is but a reflection of the whole. Things in the world are greatly out of balance. The Hopi word *koyaanisqatsi* means "world out of balance"; it is a state that requires a change in your way of being, and opening to a new way of perceiving. Envision the New Earth, where we live in harmony and recognize our interdependence, a world where ideas are shared and not held in the storehouse of greed in the name of profit. Envision a world where love is not bartered, but given openly and freely, with no conditions or expectations.

In times of dynamic change we are afforded the opportunity to take stock, organize, and clean house. Free yourself from harmful influences. Correct negative behavior and thoughts, and remove negative people and situations from your life. Take time to retreat, where you will rest, meditate, take long walks, and learn new things. Each day light your inner fire and extend the light of loving-kindness to all sentient beings. This is the medicine that heals from within.

29. KAN THE PIT/DANGER

䷜

Above Kan — gorge, precipice, snare; the taking of risks, the danger of swift-flowing waters

Below Kan — gorge, precipice, snare; the taking of risks, the danger of swift-flowing waters

The wisdom

You stand at the edge of the pit
of transformation.
In it lie all your fears.
The beneficial choice is to confront them;
Ignore them and you'll be swept away.
Dive in!

You are in transition now and can no longer rest on your laurels, falling back on your gifts of beauty, talent, intelligence, health, abundance, cleverness, or a silver tongue, which in the past have served you well and allowed you to move through difficulties with aplomb. The situation is different now. What you are coming up against is your primal material, the building blocks of life itself. You know it is here by the feeling deep within. This is the fire in the belly.

Your awareness is sharpened by the impending danger as you stand on the edge of an abyss. Your first impulse is to deny that this metaphorical pit is real. And when the awareness finally hits you in the gut, you would prefer to just let it sit awhile so you can come back to it later when you're not feeling so much pressure and responsibility. Having faced recent difficulties and challenges, you say, "Look at what I've just been through"—the loss, the breakup, the difficult decisions, the confrontation with the heaviness of the past. Nevertheless, through your diligence in making the changes that have allowed you to grow thus far you have entered an arena where your primal self is showing, and you're being called to address your basic beliefs and emotions. It feels dangerous, and it is.

The situation before you is governed by the elementals, the Earth's forces and energetics as inhabited by the nature beings who belong to them. The correct action is to avoid falling into the pit of the past, where you would revert to the confusion and doubts that have impeded your journey before. Now, gather your strength and confront the danger, whether it involves a relationship, a business, your art, or your health. As you bravely deconstruct the danger you will find it's not the scary ogre you thought it was. This is a transitional period where you can trust that you will be guided in working for the greater good by following what you know to be correct, compassionate, and fair.

> Opposition and danger
> When confronted head-on
> Will release the spiritual warrior
> And thus alleviate all fears.

Do not allow fear, self-righteousness, or the chattering monkey mind to take you off the path of what you know to be correct, tempting you to react to all the usual triggers. This transition has you at the threshold of what you have dreamed of and desired. The fears and doubts shaking your foundation are a sign that you're in the right place at the right time.

Once you have faced your fears, you'll be free to enter the arena of recognition, where success and satisfaction await you. This will create an aura of charisma around you, the magical force that is the law of attraction.

Spirit now asks you to come to stillness and trust that what emerges from the darkness will ultimately embrace and protect you. As you face your challenges, the ego will raise doubts, saying you went the wrong way or missed the point completely. This is when the benefit is to take the eagle's-eye view and fly as high as you can. In looking down from this lofty perspective you will see that your path was perfect all along, for it brought you here, now. These challenges were inevitable; no blame. By being compassionate with yourself, you will clear away the doubts, and love will flow in.

An awesome strength awaits you at the edge of the precipice, and here you'll be asked to sacrifice many things that may have brought comfort but made you blind to what is necessary to be fully engaged in the risk of growth. Place on Earth's altar your old habits, patterns, ways of thinking, and judgments that no longer serve you or the world. In this case, these comfortable, worn-out shoes are no longer suitable for your journey to contentment and understanding. By making sacrifices in humility, you will gain honor and place in your relationships, family, and tribe.

Now is the time to be fully awake and unleash your hidden powers. Take the risk. You can do it. In fact, you've already begun.

30. LI RADIANCE/AUSPICIOUSNESS

☲☲

Above	Li	glowing light, the power of awakening
Below	Li	glowing light, the power of awakening

The wisdom

Fire on the water,
A bright omen of change

Consider the image of fire on the water: this kua is symbolic of your present situation. The fire represents your courage and resolve; the water refers to matters of the soul, your heart, your intuition. The fire clings to the heart and makes way for the new as it burns away obstacles that have kept your heart in bondage. Old belief systems and tired, ingrained societal patterns are fuel for the fire, which is illuminating the jewels of your life that have been hiding, overshadowed by the ego and obscuring the pathway to the soul's illumination.

Rituals of freedom are appropriate and necessary now. Ritual clears your vision, which will be stunning as your belief in yourself takes hold and sets you free. Set the ritual table and create ceremony. In these actions a new seriousness comes into play, and the patterns that have been holding you back are eliminated through your ritual release of doubt and shame. By deconstructing their origins, these obstacles will lose their power over you, and the energy that went to them will be liberated. Make a plan, ask for assistance if need be, and dig into your doubts as you are presented with the light of transformation.

It is a time of gathering together.
The fire reveals what has been hidden.

You are entering a cycle of change
Where all is illuminated and all is possible.

You are right where you're supposed to be with this fire raging in your belly, excited and a little scared. Use your excitement and fear to fuel the sacred fire that is building deep within. Soon the fear will lessen, and your purpose and path will be revealed.

Honoring where you've been and what you've experienced will be the benefit. Honor all sentient beings, your body and spirit, love, art, and your sense of place. Mix all with healthy dose of laughter and it will be a powerful elixir to sustain you on the journey. It's what you have learned up to this point that will feed this sacred fire that comes as a ritual cycle to enliven your spirit.

The hexagram Li represents the fire in the belly and the passion in your heart. Look to the element of fire and how it burns, clings, and releases. This is your lesson: see the element of fire as it burns away what's no longer useful. The fire's licking flames across the surface of the water—your soul—are gifts of comfort and passion, consuming the old and igniting the new and the creative.

Change the words your ego uses in an attempt to block your creativity and stop you from loving and being loved. You are in the mode of learning to receive, learning that receiving does not hurt, it inspires. Embrace and rededicate what works, and with a swift sword cut what no longer serves you. Be diligent in keeping the flames burning bright by opening to the wisdom of spirit helpers who've been standing by you all this time, waiting for you to step into the light of your truth. Share that wisdom, which will help make the world a much brighter place.

As you face old, rancid patterns and behaviors, you will be leaving suppressed, worn-out, painful alliances with family, friends, and associates, breaking the unspoken contracts that have bound you to old ways, ways that didn't leave room for you to be fully in your truth. In this way the beauty of what was etched in the original canvas of your soul is revealed, and your purpose is activated and brought front and center.

Embrace your greatness and strength. You are entering a time when you can deliver clarity to your tribe and family, who also yearn for the light. Be assured that you are the one to deliver this light in all its brilliance. During times such as this, live in the fullness of being incarnate at this momentous time of change in which you can bring in the light for the greater good. In this way your light will not wain, and you will remain a steadfast spiritual warrior.

The feelings that are stirring within are powerful, and by marshalling them you will come to remember who you truly are. See yourself in your magnificence as you step out from behind the shadows in a glorious garb of light for all to see.

The unexpected is here, bringing together what belongs together.

31. XIAN CONJUNCTION

䷞

Above Dui — grow, harvest; pleasant, free, unhindered
Below Gen — quiet mountain; unshakable, steady, firm, and still

The wisdom

United in spirit:
That which belongs together
Is coming together;
That which does not belong together
Will be torn apart.

Mutual attraction can be exciting as well as beneficial to all concerned, whether in civil society, business, politics, friendship, or in matters of the heart. The work that you've done in your inner and outer worlds is near completion. With diligence, loose ends and scattered thoughts and actions are now coming together. There are awesome and mysterious forces at work these days, and they're propelling you toward your companions of, and your position in, destiny.

Projects and people who will attract you, and you them, are coming into view. For situations to come to fruition you will benefit by approaching them with honor, integrity, and respect. In romance, men are to proceed gently toward a desired mate. Yield as wheat stalks do when a gentle wind blows, remaining rooted, strong, and supple, with no desire to dominate. For the goddess, be open, inviting, and receptive when you want to join with another, and project your good intentions. For you both, be modest and leave room for discovery. Walk slowly and allow time to see the beauty of the journey. Courtship is correct at this time, as there is an opening to bring in joyful union and to renew unions that have been lying fallow, where the magic of romance has been ignored and not honored.

Deconstruct your fears and doubts and trust your intuition without trying to control outcomes. Be clear in your intent—honest, without ego, judgment, or ambition—and the disparate parts will easily come together. In this way you will have a beneficial influence on those who are walking the path with you. Speaking your truth will draw the right people and situations to you. In turn, this same truth will cause the ones who do not resonate with you to be turned away. These are auspicious times.

In love, commerce, and in spirit, leave space for others to move freely, at their own pace and rhythm, as together you move toward one another and your common goals. This is freedom—freedom for you to be yourself, and freedom for others to be so as well. In this way you show honor and respect, for yourself and others. This in turn sets you up to experience synchronicity, in which everything in your sphere of influence unfolds as it should, when it should. Do not doubt that you are in the right place at the right time, where success and joy can grow beyond anything you could have ever imagined.

If you are considering an involvement with another person, either romantic, creative, or professional, closely observe their behavior in both tranquil and stressful times, and then observe how you yourself feel when you're around that person. If you feel good, you may choose to join with that person. If you do not experience positive feelings, consider that you've been informed by your intuition that you should reject that person or situation.

Embrace the woman
Wise word
The way is open

This rather obscure statement from the original translation of the I Ching is actually referring to this very time. It is saying embrace the universal yin changes that are at play. The wheel of change, change for the greater good, is rolling with the massive energies of these times, times of great and proper change. That is why Earth's peoples are feeling that they are moving rapidly, that the days and weeks are getting shorter and shorter—and they *are.* It's an amorphous idea, this bizarre concept we call time: it really has nothing to do with what we've been conditioned to believe it is. In relating instead to the concept of *timing* you will benefit from finding your point of stillness in order to flow with the changes that are manifesting in the collective.

Don't deny the excitement and the passion you're feeling for another person, a creative project, an idea, or a grand vision. These feelings are arising from your karmic path, your destiny, and from the collective consciousness. It's Spirit's way of getting your attention, signaling that we are entering a new timing frequency, the natural frequency of the cosmos—whether that dinosaur of a sixteenth-century mechanical device known as the Gregorian calendar, designed to keep you at your post nine to five, knows it or not. You can embrace it or run for the hills. Xian, this hexagram, suggest the former, as the latter means stagnation and the ultimate death of the spirit.

Embrace the changes coming your way and allow synchronicity and the laws of attraction to effortlessly bring peace, love, and blessings. They are all here as archetypes. Those who deny it will be left without guidance and will spin in confusion from the overload of cosmic energy that will hit them like falling temple walls while they stand still and resist. Not pleasant.

The appropriate action at this time is to flow with the changes as you follow, with respect, the laws of attraction. Everyone has an opportunity now, whether they know it or not. Many will *not* be willing to ride the waves; in this case, respectfully step aside and allow them their decision to forego the gifts of healing and advancement that these times are bringing. Instead, focus on uniting with others of like heart and spirit. Set your intention for the greater good and treat all your activities, in all areas of your life, as sacred. It is the knowing and activation of the sacred that allows the situations and the people who will benefit you to find you.

We are each obligated, simply by being in this matrix, to make the best of these times. Know for certain that it is in the perfect order of things to be passionate about what is unfolding within you and around you.

32. HENG PERSEVERING

Above Zhen shake, arousal, inspiration
Below Sun root, foundation, tree

The wisdom

Thunder and wind:
You are not dislodged
In the face of adversity;
Perseverance brings benefits.

The Yi Jing is known as the "Book of Changes," and change is on the wind for you at this time: darkness will give way to light, and light will give way to darkness. The teaching of Heng is this: no matter how powerful the change, remain constant and true to yourself, to the spirit of selflessness you have cultivated through your good works. You have come to a place where you have developed compassion for all and have entered into service for the greater good. If you find either of these lacking, simply move into action. This will be of great benefit to you, your tribe, and your community.

The lines that comprise Heng speak of what has grown from a seed and become strong and vital. Consider that the seed would not have fallen and become the mighty tree had the wind not dislodged it and carried it to the Earth, the fertile Mother, where it would persevere and grow.

Thunder and wind are bound together. Thunder comes to shake us awake; wind blows to exact change. These are universal truths. When you are fully awake and you actively salve the wounds of spirit and self, you can lovingly observe your situation and thus remain constant during times of upheaval and disruption. After all, compassion begins at home.

We have entered the time of the great turning. What's happening on a global level is being projected in very personal ways as well. It may be in the attitudes of those you work with or are in relationship with; it may relate to your projects or your health or some aspect of your physical identity; it may relate to how you see yourself in the world, your true purpose. Whatever the particulars of the changes you are feeling, the benefit will be to courageously take the risk necessary to make dynamic these changes. This will bring order and harmony to your personal situation.

Thunder is heard;
Wind whips around you.
Remain steady and true.

Do not stop or change your principles on the path to completion. To adapt to the changes swirling around you, grace and tenaciousness are called for. This is a time to let the beauty of your hard-won self-awareness and your loving nature shine as you move with the rhythm of the Earth, harmonizing with her seasons as you heal and grow. Cultivate the soil and plant in the spring; nurture in the summer; harvest in the fall; and rest and renew in the winter. This is what it means to dance to the rhythm of Gaia. You are Gaia's child—slow down and listen to her. Your dance will arise spontaneously as your heart remains open and steady.

Heng can be translated both as persevering and duration, continuance in time. It seems to contain a conflicting message: it says change, but at the same time, don't change. This paradoxical statement is a valuable exercise in contemplation and will bring forth truths that are held in mystery and not yet known to you.

When you are met with obstacles you will be best served by altering your strategy. However, in so adapting you should not change your essential self. Stay in your integrity and dignity. In this way you will be able to act from and for the highest good to benefit all concerned.

It's stressful to risk and make big changes, so be sure to take time to rest and renew. As a spirit warrior go with strength and compassion and adjust to what is happening around you. It is in this time of renewal, looking inward and remembering who you really are, that love, abundance, and success will be found and placed at your doorstep.

To reach a harmonious state of being with the conditions and challenges that have been foisted on you, give yourself permission to remember who you are, embracing the realization of how far you've come and the good works you've done. As you find compassion for yourself, actively cultivate compassion for others and for Earth and all her sentient beings. It is from this place of strength and loving-kindness that you will see through to the heart of your situation. In so seeing, you will be able to move easily beyond any obstacles on your path to achieve your goals.

Flow with change and do not cling to the shore as the river carries you toward your destiny. Honor the good works of your companions and yourself. In this way you will make the world a better place for all and give respect to Gaia, the ever-present force that binds all sentient beings together in a harmonic of love.

Do not allow your light to be dimmed by any chaos or fear around you. Shine like the sun at midday. Live consciously and *be love.* Be a being of humor and light. Tell a joke and laugh at yourself when you're feeling the sometimes silly predicament of being a human being.

33. DUN RETIRING

Above	Qian/Gan	dynamic forward motion
Below	Gen	stop, still, quiet

The wisdom

Dark forces are gathering;
This is a time of protection;
Purify body, mind, and spirit
And with a considered plan, retreat.

You have garnered attention by your recent personal accomplishments and advancements. Normally it would seem that it's time to use this as fuel to move further toward your goals. It looks that way—but it is not such a time. Do not fall prey to the temptation of ego to take the good vibes, notice, and acclaim given to you by your tribe and community to move further toward your goal of love and abundance. It seems energetically more than possible, but paradoxically you will now benefit from retreat. Make a plan and stick to it.

As a moth is drawn to a flame, you are attracting unwanted and potentially negative situations. You have done nothing wrong; in fact, it is quite the opposite. Knowing this, with confidence and good planning, move away from seduction and flattery. Let it appear that you are holding place and are using the recent acclaim and notice to advance—let it *look* that way, but in reality be in inner stillness as you protect that which is yours. You need a break, a moment to consider where you've been and how far you've come.

It will be a delicate maneuver to make it look like you are moving gracefully forward all the while you are moving toward retreat.

Here is where strategy is important. Conflict is just beginning to show itself. Do not engage; you cannot win this battle right now. Move without your audience, tribe, and associates noticing that you have gone into a quiet stillness and are, in that stillness, gathering your powers and strength. And when you do, you'll come back with such a force and with such great light that all who in the past might have tried to control, obstruct, or manipulate you will be in awe and wonderment as to where this energy blast came from. This will please Spirit and set you in the right place to overcome the difficulties and obstacles that are now appearing.

The benefit now is to move into recovering from your various exertions in solitude, into a time of meditative contemplation of what lies ahead. Go to a place known only by you, to your inner self, that peaceful place where the resounding echoes of the inner voice of wisdom, fate, and clarity reside and the clattering voices recede into the background.

A covert retreat such as this, on its face, may look and feel like deception. You've worked hard not to be deceptive, not to hide your worth and to be seen as truthful. You have done well, but now you must be strategic. Strategy is not deceptive or dishonest; it's a necessary aspect of progress and process. To move forward you will benefit by first moving inward.

> In retreat there is strength and subtlety.
> Do not set the record straight
> Or try to make things right.
> Don't go there now, it won't work.

It would be folly to confront, compromise, or try to power through the obstacles that have been placed on your path, as your words would not be heard, valued, or respected. Instead, take the attitude of the sacred mountain and hold still. This does not mean do nothing and just sit around and wait. What the hexagram Dun is saying is that by making a well-timed and covert retreat, you will be able to gather your strength and nurture a vision that will allow you to formulate a brilliant, well-thought-out plan that you can activate upon your return. Above all, refrain from making any announcements that you are going into retreat.

Keep in mind that while in retreat you will formulate a plan. To all but your most trusted confidants of the heart, it will seem like you never went anywhere.

Note well and do not be naïve: there is brewing a battle between the dark and the light. Let it play out and do not engage. If you do engage, the dark forces will swallow you up, leaving you confused, disempowered, weak, depressed, and angry. Instead, let the drama play out; allow the dragon to eat its own tail.

In retreat you will find purification. You will be able to think more clearly, love more freely, and regain the mantle of self-confidence and those longed-for feelings of inner peace. Any feelings of impotence will disappear.

Make your retreat joyous. Find new experiences and explore new ideas. Let your eyes and ears find new feasts that delight. Cultivate compassion and still your mind. In retreat and stillness, Spirit will find you and bring valued teachings from the masters who have sent their envoys to assist in the return of the light to our planet. They will come with compassion and great kindness, nurturing the emerging and oh-so-delicate inception of the Golden Age to come. Together with your fellow pilgrims both known and unknown, harmonize with the alchemical formula of love, kindness, and compassion. Hold this vision for yourself and for all as you contemplate, in retreat, the New Earth that will emerge. It is in contemplating thus that clarity will emerge. And when you finally do come out of your retreat you will be dazzling in your confidence, a brilliant, shining star.

Never doubt the value of being of service and having a clear worldview. This is vital at this time of transition, a time in which you are fully engaged. By joining your intentions with others of like mind, you will join the New Earth tribe. Together we will stand in the light to welcome the dawn of simplicity, kindness, and compassion.

Hold close and dear the ones you love and who love you. The energetic shift that is in progress is laced with love and compassion. This is what you've been waiting for, a time of remembering who you truly are, an incarnate spirit having a human experience.

You are the one you have been waiting for, and we are the ones we have been waiting for.

34. DA ZHUANG GREAT POWER

䷡

Above	Zhen	thunder, shaking, excitement, inspiration
Below	Quin/Gan	Heaven, Spirit power

The wisdom

The spirit of the joyous dancer has arrived.
It has come in support
As you enter a cycle
Of strength and correctness.

The awaited and predicted changes have begun in earnest. This applies to you and to the world. Much will occur during this period of dynamic change as we shift to a higher harmonic. It is correct to approach the coming changes with a renewed commitment to personal and societal transformation for the betterment of all sentient beings.

In your actions the benefit will be to change the way you've been thinking about your plan, your place in the universe, and how you can be of service. Thinking differently will allow your words to flow as if from a fountain that has been still for eons and now flows freely, like water in a mountain stream, bubbling forth with strength and lyricism. As you hear your own words it will be as if you are witnessing your own mind as you speak from your intuition. Conduct yourself with honor and integrity as you enter this time of assured success. Have no fear of keeping your standards high and being seen; you are safe.

In this cycle call on your sense of humor as you join with the cosmic energies, which have a grand sense of humor. This attracts the spirit dancers who are your companions on the path to completion and success. The benefit now is to embrace this transformative cycle with thoughtfulness and flexibility. The spiral of energy before you will lead to what is greater than great, a wholeness that will serve as a launching pad as you accelerate on your path for the greater good. Listen with rapt attention as Gaia invokes her messages of change. In these times of flux some of these messages will not be so pleasant. With no fear, find the symbolism in these dispatches from Mother Earth; as you dissect them they will point the way to the path ahead.

As above, so below. With humor see the irony in the crazy ways of thinking in the old upside-down world, where white is black and black is white. A sense of humor will smooth the ride. Laugh well and laugh loud—be the seed in the tribe who brings a joyous mood as you join in celebration and gratitude for endings and beginnings. Then come to stillness as you seek the inner sage in a momentary pause to fully realize what's happening.

An energetic package such as you are about to receive comes with responsibility. The ego would seize the availability of Great Power and run with it, trying to control and change things for its sole benefit. Dismiss the influence of the ego, as your mastery is now more powerful than ever before. Misuse of power is an easy trap to fall into, and the veil between the dark and the light is very thin. So it is of utmost importance that you spot any tendency to misuse this energy, and instead move with integrity and compassion as your guiding principles. If you ignore the universal laws, the misuse of Great Power would lead to loss of what you have been working so hard for.

In this cycle step up and insist on the respect and abundance you have wanted and deserve. In business, receive your fair share and reach to new heights; as an artist, request the place where you wish to be seen and heard; in love, move toward what or whom you thought was unattainable; in your intimate life, open the door to sensual connection that you have closed.

> Fear not the thunder.
> The great force of nature is wise.
> It is your wake-up call.

Thunder in Heaven, says the oracle—you are not afraid, you are awake! Correctness and working for the greater good is the only way to handle this potent timing. It is the Earth's rising frequency in times of great change, signaling a return to Eden both in concept and in reality. All who realize this truth will be embraced by Spirit. Be awake and conscious of this realization, and this time will be confusing no more.

As one cycle ends you are presented with a glorious beginning. From this point on, the way forward will be your creation, your novel approach as to how you see and activate your part in the scheme of things. This will lead to good fortune and peace of mind.

Nurture the spirit within and be empathetic to your fellow pilgrims on the path. Be of loving heart, with kindness and generosity. In this way you will benefit by making safe the way for your fellows. The choice for change is a choice to embark on the road less traveled. It will be lonely at times, so disembowel the old isolationist patterns and adhere to the principle of oneness, the interconnected whole. When the question of purpose arises, the answer will not come from some revelatory Orson Welles voice from above; it is already answered and will speak to the spiritual warrior through the siren song of the soul. There is great joy in stillness. In sacred silence, listen to the song.

Progress is a certainty at this time. Clearly observe yourself to make sure you are being honorable, compassionate, and kind, with a lightness of being that is correct for who and where you are. And have no fear. Remember who you are, and in that magnificence you will travel on the wings of truth and be a beacon of light for all to see.

35. JIN FLOURISHING

Above Li	radiance, fire; brightness that brings clarity and passion
Below Kun	center of Earth; that on which everything rests; the basis of all things

The wisdom

Great progress is on the horizon;
A powerful force awaits you.
Come to stillness and listen.
Wise words will be there for you.

Make the choice to be at your best and fullest at this, your finest hour. The time to move into action is here and now. This is a time of rapid progress.

At this turn of the wheel you will benefit by hatching a plan of action. Once you've made a well-considered plan you will be backed by a powerful force coming from unseen spirit helpers who have brought you to this moment of evolutionary advancement. Their guidance will come when you go within.

You are in a potent time of advancement. This is a time when you can benefit society. Strive for fairness in situations where you hold power or influence. Honor those who work with you and for you. If you are solo in your craft or art, honor the dancing spirit who comes as a muse to enliven you and tickle your fancy. Make a relationship with this spirit, and it will soothe you and bring solace to mind and heart. Don't forget how you got here and who has been your support, and recognize those who have blazed the trail for you. Honor your mentors and guides; give them praise and honor. You are gaining an abundance of power, influence, love, and prosperity; share this with your tribe. In this way you are signaling your gratitude and eschewing the ego, and gratitude is the catalyst in the alchemical mixture that delivers us from doubt, fear, and avarice.

Coming mercifully into your life now is a very powerful energetic force. It is a currency of sorts—spend it wisely. Be guided by compassion as you examine your patterns of behavior, identifying that which has not served you in the recent past and if continued would surely create obstacles to further progress. Replace these outworn patterns with new, positive ways of thinking and being. The words you think are more powerful than the words you say, so correct and change self-talk when it speaks of unworthiness, guilt, or revenge.

> Inner stillness is crucial now.
> In stillness the voice of the Higher Self is heard.
> Look to your practice for connecting.
> Free yourself from judgment and criticism.

What's being presented to you now is fresh and new, and is imbuing you with confidence and strength. Power such as this can be a tricky thing, though. The way to handle it is to make a sacrifice: Let go of old habits and friends or associates who have turned their back to you. Gift portions of your abundance to those in need. Speak up in behalf of those who are powerless. Your abundance can also be expressed in words of kindness that you gift along the way. You may choose to gift material goods such as clothing or books that have served you. With an open heart and an open door, both literally and figuratively, be an active member of your community and tribe.

You are perfectly positioned and have prepared and practiced well. Have no doubts about this. Accept fully that you are in the right place at the right time. But just being in right place is not enough now—you must activate this earned gift of strength and influence with an equal dose of compassion, dignity, and kindness. This will please Spirit and open many doors that have previously been closed or missed. Spirit is with you and watching and assisting you in finding your direction. After all, it is Spirit that led you out of the darkness and into the light.

Flourishing is signaling a beautiful, full journey for you and your family, tribe, and associates, paving the way for progress in all matters. Make no mistake, there will be difficulties and obstacles on journeys such as this; this is in the natural order of things. Progress always breeds challenges, and you will benefit by meeting them head-on. Be certain you are not hiding your truth or trying to be "reasonable" in dealing with the angst that might arise. To insure continuing progress and peace of mind, be grateful, cherish the love all around you, and return it by being generous with your affection. Plan a fiesta or gather friends together for a celebration of life. Through it all, remain centered through your spiritual or physical practice. This will insure your equanimity on this bizarre adventure of being incarnate at this time on Earth.

Open your mind and heart to the art and ideas of the indigenous peoples of your geography or ancestry; go to them and listen to the soothing and familiar messages that have come through the ages. Open your eyes as well as your ears and hear the secrets and see the visions waiting for you. The ancestors, whether your direct antecedents or not, have left coded messages in the great storehouse of knowledge that are waiting to be discovered. They are signposts for the world's current residents that can lead to peace and prosperity for all.

Look around you: in the midst of chaos, the New Earth is dawning. With diligence and compassion for all sentient beings, we can join as one with Gaia to usher in a time of peace and goodwill.

36. MING I HIDING THE LIGHT

䷣

Above K'un Earth, receptive
Below Li fire, light

The wisdom Caution is advised.
Do not show your strength.
Keep your light hidden.
Dark forces feed on light.

While developing your inner strength and working for your own betterment and the good of all you have become vulnerable in ways that are not familiar to you. Therefore, you must become fully awake and brutally honest to defeat the negativity around you. There are subtle attacks rooted in jealousy or resentment trying to worm their way into your life right now. The benefit is to fly low. Take the risk of looking to your shadow. At times we must embrace our shadow self, the deep recesses of the subconscious, for there is found a reserve of energy not often used, an advisor of sorts, a protector even. If you have the courage to wrestle with your own shadow, making a preemptive strike on your unconscious dark side, getting to know it intimately and thereby bringing it into the light, you lessen your personal share of the load of the world's evil. From the shadow self, keenly observe the situation. Shadow behavior seeks out the same, like a round peg in a round hole, so the shadow contains a potent form of self-knowledge being reflected back to you.

These times clearly show the obvious difference between the light and the dark. Know this and contain your light. Continue to develop, but not in the open. These are difficult times when you are confronted with danger or obstacles on the path. It would be useless to confront these negative forces. Remain calm and let it seem that you don't notice their divisive influence as they strike out or try to stop you. Just hold steady with the knowledge that this time of hardship will bring self-knowledge that will serve you well when it's appropriate to step out of the wings and into the spotlight.

Do not let evil know that you recognize it for what it is. Branding darkness only gives it power, and that power would be taken from your own reserves. Retreat is not what's called for either, as retreat now would empower the opposition. The benefit is to stand steady and make it *appear* that you are oblivious to what is obvious—a delicate balancing act for sure, but a smart tactic for survival.

Inwardly, stand mightily on your path. If you were to give up your position, you would lose the advances you have made from all your emotional and spiritual work. If you confront the negative forces, be it a person, a nasty situation, or a major delay, you would show too much of yourself and the conflict would suck your energy, leaving you vulnerable to real injury, either physical or psychic. This is instead the time to be strong and powerful yet not show your light. In this way you will maintain your inner strength, combined with a sense of self-confidence and even humor. Yes, humor, because in many ways there is a comic veneer to this obvious play for power and control over you. Withhold revealing the irony you perceive and know that stillness is of the greatest benefit at this time.

The light of hope and faith
Has sunk into the Earth

And cannot be seen;
The treasure is thus hidden
From thieves.

When there is danger on the path, be it in family, tribe, an institution, finances, commerce, health, or in travel, now is *not* the time to try and fix it by showing your light. Your light is the result of having done your work and having gathered information and strength through diligent work for your own and the greater good. The beneficial and correct action to take during this time is to stay out of the fray. There is a teaching in early Chinese writings that says: A calling bird will summon you at the correct time and will open a new and glorious cycle for you to gain the freedom, love, and abundance that waits. Be still and listen for the sweet song of the calling bird. Never doubt that it will come.

When a dark force seems to be entering your business, health, or a relationship, the ego says to step up and try to beat it down. Ming I, this kua, gives the message that this is not the proper time for such action. Don't let your analytical mind take over and tempt you to figure out a way to defeat the challenge. That would be an error of great magnitude. Be seen as gentle and compassionate, for if you were to go on the attack you would only feed the dark forces; they would gain even more strength and would obstruct your progress for a very long time.

In confinement, whether self-imposed or not, is where your creativity can flower. The sage King Wen, many thousands of years ago, wrote the Yi Jing, the classic that the I Ching is drawn from, while hiding from his enemies and mourning his father's death. The time to shine like the sun at midday is coming, but for now chill and let the darkness pass. Very soon it will be safe to continue shining your beauty and light. This is one of the most powerful lessons in the I Ching, a lesson once learned will be your medicine in this dualistic world of yin and yang, darkness and light. Do not avoid the darkness; see it, know it, and let it run its course. In stillness you are safe; in the action of confronting it you are in danger. Let love lead the way inside and embrace stillness. From this, all will be made clear.

37. CHIA JEN THE GROUP

Above	Sun	wind
Below	Li	fire

The wisdom

The opportunity to join with others
is immanent.
This will be of great benefit.
Your actions now predict our future.

Your life path has been filled with many tasks, plans, hopes, and dreams. You've been operating on your own. You've found strength and some confidence on the journey, yet there has been an aching loneliness that has felt like a blanket dimming all that you do and all that you feel. In the West this state is often confused with depression, but in this case it is not that. The truth in the concept that we are all one should be considered as you are called to join a group, community, or family. A joining such as this will allow you to accomplish and improve all that you've worked for and held close.

To be in harmony when moving into a new clan or group, your behavior will set the tone. You will benefit by being in integrity and honor in all that you say and do—at this time and at any time. For a group to function in harmony there needs to be clarity around responsibilities and the strict recognition of traditional ways of thinking. It will be of benefit to make a solid plan that guides all toward love and respect for one another in the group. Any gossip, bitterness, or resentment will cause the group to splinter and will not allow goals to be met. Make sure each person is able to use their strengths in the group and not asked to do that which is outside their knowledge or skills. Follow the plan with diligence, knowing that you are honoring the soul of the group and yourself. It is within community where great growth is fostered and maintained.

If you find that you are in a place of leadership in the group you will be of greatest service by doing what you say you will do and being an example of what you speak or teach to others. Encourage others to do the same. If you or someone in the group has bit off more than they can chew, let them know there is no shame in speaking up and changing direction or processes.

Right now in our world we could make a very long list of what's not in harmony—in the way we treat the environment, in our political system, in our economics, in our social caste system. It is this clash of frequencies that you're feeling as disharmony and agitation. It can all seem so overwhelming, and yet you know you cannot bury your head in the sand. You know that the true benefit is to act. The world can only change when we each look within. The message "peace begins with me" is to be recognized as an alchemical code signifying correct thinking and behavior. Peace is a nonverbal language that can be practiced by all, and in the presence of a peaceful, nonviolent being the essence of peace is experienced automatically.

> The ability to bring great change
> Lies within self and clan;
> The power to solidify
> And make the change long-lasting
> Lies within the community.

A wise leader of a clan understands that it is the yin principle that supports the open and positive movement of the people. The feminine element does not push its way to the front to initiate change. Effective change comes from within. As Lao Tzu says, "To lead the people, walk behind them."

This kua is both magical and realistic in its teaching. When followed with complete integrity you will be able to initiate changes that will move the group toward progress. This, ironically, is accomplished in nonaction—the nonaction of being humble, loving, steady, honest, and sincere. If you say what you will do, do what you say. In this simplicity is a powerful force propelling you to serve the greater good.

Consider the I Ching as a code for living. It is composed of words, and those words, together and individually, are code. Learn the lesson, use the code. Meditate on the words *grace, love, compassion, affection, respect, honor,* and *kindness.* Incorporate these words in all that you do and say, in every action and decision.

38. KUI POLARIZING

Above Li radiance, brightness, fire
Below Dui open, free, unhindered

The wisdom

In the maelstrom of polarization
You are not heard.
Transformation is at hand;
Trust nothing familiar.

You are moving forward. Good offers, tempting ones, have come your way. However, doubt comes as you ask, *Will my decisions serve me and my future?* It seems that your mind is pulling one way and your heart, your traditional values, another. Yet this is not a time of either/or; it's about the blending of opposites, which will ease the rumbling in your head and the tension in your gut.

There are friendships or relationships that have drifted out of harmony. Who is right and who or what is correct? It's of no matter. These are only misunderstandings. If there is blame, be willing to take the blame. There will only be resolution in small matters.

These are times when decisions must be made. Do you stay, do you go, do you sign the contract, renegotiate it, or let it go completely? The only way to find the correct path is to ascertain whether it's your passion, your bliss. Look carefully at your options so that your decision does not put you in bondage to old, unfulfilling ways of being that are all too familiar. Fully examine your situation from all angles and move outside the norm and the traditional, established ways and old ways of thinking and behaving. It is in this place, outside the normal, that passion lies. Passion is the element needed to assist you in creating a workable blend of intellect and knowledge, without judgment or fear of loss.

> Heart versus mind.
> Tension stretches reason to its limits.
> Fate is questioned.
> Trust passion.

The ego would tell you that it must be a certain way. It says, *Conform to the established order, don't stand out, don't be eccentric, and for heaven's sake, don't be different!* Within the message of Kui is the teaching that now is the time to *not* adhere to the old rules. You will find a solution by being outrageous and eccentric, whether in art, commerce, or social interaction; whether in intimate, family, or tribal relationships. The fire of passion is yours for the taking, always there, waiting as a trusted ally to serve you in moving toward the greater good. In trusting your passion you can cut through the old ways to achieve clarity and the radiance of an open consciousness that will lead you, step-by-step, to a crystal-clear view of your situation.

Situations such as what is before you now do not happen often in life. Drop the protection, guilt, fear, and shame and let it in. You deserve it, and you will not be eaten or embarrassed, you will be en-lightened—meaning you will remember who you truly are and be unburdened and filled with light. This is a grand gift, and the teaching is real; seize it before it changes form and you are left grasping at air with tears in your eyes. Realizing this gift, this opportunity, will gladden your heart and bring clarity and peace to your mind, body, and spirit.

You may find that recently you rejected an opportunity for change or rejected a "crazy" idea or a person who invited you in.

It's not too late—in fact, the consideration you gave the situation then will serve you now. This is a time of progress, yet it seems that the things most vital for progress have been feeling unclear, and you've had trepidations about making a commitment to move forward with the coming tide. This is because you have either denied the truth in recent teachings and life lessons, or you have not comprehended or allowed another's point of view to be received. Recall the opportunity that was offered and try it on for size. It may fit or it may not—that's not the point. The point is that you are taking divergent feelings, points of view, the dark *and* the light, and combining them in such a way that it makes a mix of emotions and intellectual truths that when combined become an unstoppable force. And what you need now is just that—an unstoppable force.

Consider this: the opposites you are observing before you are not obstacles. They have been put in your path to wake you up, to get your attention. The pesky, negative side of the ego that abhors change would have you stay in your position without passion forever, wallowing in old, established ways and stale patterns of behavior that close your mind and heart to the possibilities of growth and renewal of your most important relationship, the one with yourself.

There seems to be contradiction in almost every situation you are being presented with—relationships, art, business, health, and the spiritual path. Most likely it's a combination of these things that has driven you to distraction, and being distracted at this point in your progress is the last thing you need or want.

You need not depend on anyone else to make decisions for you, no matter how close they are to you or how deep the trust is or how much power or influence they can exert. You are on your own in this one. Take advantage of that and enter the arena. Do not let any decisions be made for you, either outright or through another's influence. Pull your sword of passion, your reality, and strike down any movement, idea, or situation that stands between you and your happiness. It's a risk, but this advancement requires risk.

Dualism such as what you are experiencing in these times is part of the hero's journey, and you are that hero warrior. On the outside it may look like you are indecisive as you carefully examine all angles of your situation. It doesn't matter how it looks to others as you consider and seek the balance between light and dark, yin and yang, life and death; it is that serious at this time. Embrace the dualistic forces that are confronting you. You will gain much knowledge and infinite strength by making and embracing this commitment.

Take these teachings to heart and make small, considered, even covert movements as you commit to the elemental nature of this part of your life path. Stay in your integrity in all decisions. Have compassion for those who have tried to block or consume you, and stay in the knowing that you are discovering who you truly are.

39. JIAN OBSTRUCTION/DIFFICULTIES

Above Kan gorge, test, a critical time; tread with caution
Below Gen obstacle; quiet motionlessness

The wisdom

Abundance in view,
Just out of reach.
Identify the obstruction,
Embrace the teaching:
Adverse conditions are a practitioner's true wealth.

On the road to enlightenment, obstructions often seem to appear from out of nowhere. You've done your work, affirmed the correct way, yet an old, familiar, nagging voice arises, causing doubt. If you allow it, it can instill enough fear and shame to take you off your path toward a well-deserved abundance of spirit and love in your life. At this pivotal moment the ego is flinging out old ideas at you, triggering all your old patterns to challenge you. You have been here before and know how to deconstruct these kinds of obstacles. You have done it time and time again. But in your quest you have missed a vital component: compassion for yourself. No blame—your suffering is a signal that freedom is just beyond the veil.

You have been conscious of operating from a generous and loving light within, and this is good. What you missed or may have forgotten is that some old emotional obstacles still exist. Not only do they exist, as you have evolved and gained strength, so have the obstacles. You will find that the ego is trying to make it seem like these blocks are enormous, so big you'd better dive under the covers and hide, or better yet, says the ego, cut and run. But no need to hide or run—you are facing nothing more than the soul's shadow, which has emerged from the deep. Stay steady now. This aspect of your shadow self cannot withstand the wisdom you have garnered through your commitment to being honest and congruent, to saying what you mean and meaning what you say. The truth will set you free—it really is that simple. You will not be blocked if you move with dignity into the heart of the matter and see yourself for who you truly are—strong, wise, compassionate, and fearless—all the while you walk and talk, and do not manipulate, your truth.

> It is time to be outrageous.
> With passion and inner fire,
> Open the mouth of truth;
> Demand that the truth within yourself be revealed.

The truth, in this case, is what is found inside you, in the wisdom and compassion of your true self. It's been there all along, waiting for you to claim it. You have been here before; the difference is that this time you are accessing the wisdom reminder contained in this hexagram. The teaching of Jian comes to bring you to the place of truth within yourself, the truth being that you'd better change your way of thinking lest you end up being hobbled by the shadow self again.

In the last go-round of addressing obstacles you learned a great deal, but you missed a few things lurking in the shadows. These little devils of the negative ego are now puffing themselves up, trying to appear huge, but in fact they are nothing more than bits of the shadow self coming into the full consciousness of the wisdom mind. Don't let fears or doubts take over at this stage of the game; these are merely vestiges of the old conditioning you've been diligently working to identify and slough off. Those patterns were weakened, no doubt, but they're tricky. You've taught them a little too well. In fact, it's a good thing these fears are bubbling to the surface now, to allow you to fortify your intention to live for the greater good, and to let go of fears and doubts once and for all.

If what you are feeling is an obstacle toward completion or a joining, consider that if a boulder were to roll off the mountain into a stream, the flow of water would surely be blocked. When this happens, the water doesn't fret and feel sorry for itself; it pauses. In this momentary pause, the water builds up behind the rock—which in this case is your ego—and gathers strength. And with that strength it doesn't try to move the boulder, for that would be a waste of energy. What the wisdom contained in the water does is gather itself, and with grace, flow around the boulder.

The benefit now is to begin to see difficulties and obstacles in a new way, as tests of your wisdom. Pushing the obstacle away or trying to outsmart it will only give it more strength, and it will use that strength to further hamper your journey, exhausting you in the process. Instead, use it to hone your perfection.

Take a moment to look around you to see who or what process can help you. Is it a wise sage or a trusted teacher? Is it a ceremony, a ritual, or a dance? Whatever it is, make the connection and know that there is no blame in asking for assistance; this is not weakness, it is strength.

When an obstacle blocks your path, seize the moment and dip into your energetic reservoir to disassemble it and see it for what it is. Know that the benefits of having been diligent about seeking the truth and generating loving-kindness are that they are a kind of currency you can use in situations just like this one. In this case, go into stillness and listen to the voice of your inner wise one. In this way the current obstacles will come into the light of your own recognition. Then, by opening your heart and taking a deep breath, then exhaling with intent, they will be seen as nonthreatening to your true, genuine self. Once they have been dispatched, make sure you haven't missed other obstacles lurking in the dark recesses. This is the key to long-lasting success: being aware and listening to the voice of the inner observer.

It is an acquired skill to quiet the mind in the face of difficulties and obstructions. It can only come through a commitment to practice. It can be done once you understand that all obstacles are signposts on the road, guiding you toward your true, compassionate self. As you proceed in this practice you may find you have to change the object of your desire. If this is deemed necessary, it will spell freedom—the freedom to be who you really are.

By being still, you will open the doorway to your wisdom mind. It is here, in stillness, that guidance awaits you.

40. XIE UNRAVELING

䷧

Above Zhen — shake, arouse, inspire, excite: thunder rising from the Earth

Below Kan — gorge, test, a critical time: a swift stream tearing through a chasm; proceed with caution

The wisdom

Liberation!
The heavens release rain
That has been held back.
Obstacles are washed away.
Set your intentions well.

Like a long-awaited rainfall after a lengthy drought, we are in the process of releasing old stuff that we have been sentimental about or the things that were just so sticky they wouldn't come off our fingers or the soles of our feet. The quality and quantity of energy that abounds now on Earth, which is coming directly from a rarely tapped universal storehouse, is making it possible for us to move out of the old ways of doing and being, thus opening the way to seeing the possibilities of a new way. But not just new—a revolutionary way.

The open wounds, where abuse—from internalized judgments or from society's weird, backward rules—has been heaped on you, are in line for healing and release. It is in the perfect order right now to recall all the abuse and misunderstandings of the past. In doing so you will unravel the knots that have bound you, and the world, to the past. Well, brothers and sisters, that funky old program that has been running in the background of your life is, if you so will it, about to go out the door, which stands wide open, leaving that same door open to welcome in new opportunities.

> Bitterness, guilt, and jealousy
> Are burdens too heavy for this journey.
> Pack a light bag and move on.
> Don't miss this train;
> It's the one called *Liberation.*

What in the sixties was called "flower power" was just a crack in the door. Ideas came in but did not have the force and strength to carry us all the way through. But energy is never lost; it accumulates until the next cycle. What is before us now has the focus and strength needed to affect sweeping changes, and this opportunity *must* be seized if you want to fulfill your deepest desires and move us all toward the greater good.

In one version of the tarot, the card Good Fortune shows a woman with a beautiful head of hair. It is said that she is bald in back—meaning that when luck, good fortune, or opportunity comes your way, you must grab it by the forelocks and bring it to you, because if you feel it but hesitate to go into action, it will pass you by, and there will be nothing to grab onto in back, and you will be stuck waiting for the next chance, which, sadly, may not come again for a very long time.

It is true there has been abuse—emotional, physical, and spiritual; environmental, personal, and societal. It has affected you and your journey forward. Now is the time to recognize this, to forgive yourself and release others, and be ready to seize all the good that's coming your way. Deliverance is at its beginning; be bold, take the risk.

You perceive that you've been surviving and keeping your head above water. Now is the time to swim to shore, dry off, partake of the libation that awaits you, and jump headfirst into the new opportunities that are about to be, or already are, presented. You have asked for this and now it is here. Good work, tribesperson, good work indeed!

The benefit now is to leave the abuse that has been influencing your journey—no blame or guilt. With truth, integrity, and courage you will find your situation suddenly changing for the better. Trust this magic, which is your personal power. Despite the grim picture of total control the corporate media is projecting, we are each of us, right now, in the energy of deliverance. Don't doubt it! Exercise self-love and generosity of spirit. Replace the burden of negative thoughts and feelings with loving-kindness. Have compassion for Mother Earth and all her beings. Nature will guide you in releasing your own inner wisdom. I know you have heard this call before, so now go for it and put the words of the ancient oracle into practice in your daily activities and meditation.

Trusting yourself is called for now. Trust your strength as an incarnated human microcosm at this momentous time in human history, and muster all your courage to cut the Gordian knot that has bound you to the tired old ways that have held sway for too long. The knot may have its root in your childhood; it may be from last year or from yesterday, or from the countless generations that have preceded you. Just know that the past does not exist. All we have is right now. And our now is what makes the future beautiful, as long as we fill it with loving-kindness.

You will be letting some people go, along with some old ideas and the old wounds. That is what liberation and deliverance is all about. Don't judge other people's stuff. That is theirs, not yours. Take the ride. This train is dynamic, thrilling, sexy, loving, and bright.

41. SUN — DIMINISHING AND OFFERING

Above	Gen	limit, quietness, the mountain
Below	Dui	open, easy, responsive

The wisdom

Make an offering
At the altar of all you hold dear.
Your offering
Is to be fully present.

Opportunity is rising—the opportunity to retrieve a beautiful aspect of yourself that has been hiding in the shadows, hidden from view as you strode ahead toward your goals.

You have been in the action and attitude of giving—giving love or advice to benefit your family, tribe, and relationships. Now prepare to receive, to clear the way that has been cluttered with ego, personality, and greed. You have not been wrong in these very human actions, but now a great cleanse is called for, a clearing of old ways and patterns that have held you in doubt and shame. This clearing will allow you to proceed refreshed on the road less traveled in the coming cycle.

The benefit is to have a plan spelling out what needs to shifted, retrieved, or let go of, be it a relationship, an attachment to self-importance, or the illusion of being in control. In letting go of what no longer serves you, you will leave room for new creations and to be loved for who you are, without the artifice of control or pretending to be someone you're not.

There is great benefit in creating an altar, a place to go either metaphorically or in actuality, where in stillness you can connect with the higher wisdom that's available to you. This is a psychedelic journey of sorts, one that calls on the magical hormones of the human body to open the doors that have been forever closed. It is in this space where you will know you are awake and on the road less traveled, the Medicine Path. It is at this sacred altar where you can dip into deeply held reserves of energy and power, fuel for the transformational changes that are before you.

To receive the abundance of love and peace of mind that is destined for you, the benefit is to not only clean the vessel, but to carefully scrutinize it for even the tiniest cracks in your way of thinking, and then seal those cracks. Be cautious that you are not blinded by the successes you've manifested. You will, in reflection, see that in many ways you *have* done well—that is not in question. To receive in fullness, however, Spirit asks that that you recognize and move beyond the chattering ego that is constantly looking for a way to ever so subtly tempt you to move off-track, away from the Divine.

You've been moving in many directions to achieve what you have desired, while keeping steady on your necessary daily tasks of caring for yourself and those around you. Despite all this activity there's been a lack of satisfaction. Rising up from deep within is a gnawing desire to reach for something new, something grand. In many ways it seems like this time of angst and convoluted ideas swirling around must be the worst time of all for a journey such as this, as you have been expending so much of your vital force just to get to where you are and to maintain your equilibrium while doing so. It is now that the hexagram Sun advises you to take a clear look at your situation, and then negotiate your position, paying attention to your limitations. As you proceed, with honesty and integrity as your guiding lights, make sure you stay within the boundaries of your energetic, spiritual, emotional, and physical resources. Don't let the ego push you beyond these important limits, for it's when you become exhausted that you are vulnerable to the ego's voicings of doubt and shame.

> It is a time for simple plans;
> Complexity will rob you of your resources.
> The path to success must be free and open,
> Unhindered by negative thoughts and stale beliefs.

When we see the sun diminishing at the end of day we do not mourn the sunset or feel that it's the end of life as we know it. This decline can be one of our finest moments, as we are in awe of the beauty of nature's cycles. We recognize that the end of the day is the end of a cycle, nothing more. This describes where you're at now—the end of a cycle. It's time to make an offering, prostrating, figuratively or literally, before the altar of virtue.

This time is what some call fate—a time that expresses itself in a celebratory way as you set the ego aside and let go of fears and doubts to follow Spirit, your guides, your good angels, or whatever term you use to identify the voice of higher wisdom that nurtures and advises you in this time of decrease. It's from here that good, solid boundaries can be created. These limitations will help you regulate your self-expression, which will become increasingly prescient because most of the negative voices within will be exhausted by their chattering and forced to move into silence. This is called *relief.*

So in this time of lessening of personal power, look to your virtue and act and think as simply as possible. Work only at the basic elements of your tasks; eat, drink, and think simply. Make an offering of your ego to the ones on high. This ego sacrifice may be in the form of material objects or an attitude of condescension that was just about to get you in a world of trouble.

As your energetic sun is setting, know that at nighttime you will be renewed and prepared for the eventual rising of your strength, energy, and wholesomeness. This will empower you to bring loving-kindness to your personal relationships, tribe, family, and business associations, allowing you to easily accomplish more than you had planned.

Some natural cycles can be hard to accept. When you find yourself in a time of limitations, you may worry or feel anxious. But know that this cycle is temporary and is part of the natural order. Decrease gives you an opportunity to clearly look at your life path so that you can address and correct negative thoughts and old, worn-out patterns of behavior. Rather than being something to get through, the current cycle should be considered a time of revelation and revolution that will lead to a personal renewal, leaving you clear and strong to work for your own and the greater good.

There has been much pain and suffering on our planet. Trust that we are working our way toward the time of the New Earth, when our vision for Gaia will emerge. It is up to each of us to hold the vision and keep our balance. Thus great benefit will be delivered as we act in harmony with the universal laws.

42. YI — AUGMENTING/BLESSINGS IN GREAT MEASURE

䷩

Above Sun — root/tree/foundation; standing on a firm platform to achieve a slow and nourishing penetration into the heart of the matter

Below Zhen — shake, arouse, inspire, excite; thunder rising from the Earth

The wisdom — All things are possible now.
Energies are increasing.
Be generous and ethical.
Now you will flourish.

A cycle of growth, rejuvenation, increase, development, and gain is being made available to you. By moving with integrity and compassion, seeking to benefit your entire milieu, you have arrived at the time of Blessings in Great Measure. Place no limits on your intentions, ideas, and projects. If any negative thoughts that would foul the path before you linger, swiftly correct them by applying the appropriate antidotes.

This is a time when great benefit is to be had by trusting yourself and recognizing that unseen benevolent forces are at work, amplifying growth and gain. Look to the many situations that surround you now, be it in your work, relationships, health, art, or inner development. Focus on how you want things to grow, and make changes for the greater good. Trust your intuition as to the correct actions, and move beyond doubt, judgment, or shame, and into fearlessness. You are blessed.

With an open heart, make a plan. Once you've made a commitment to your path and you apply the current energetics to the tasks at hand, prepare for the increase that is rapidly approaching. By realizing this, your activities are infused with positivity, and you will get what you want, no doubt about it.

> The harvest is coming.
> Examine your intent.
> Share the bounty, both materially and spiritually;
> Generosity and loving-kindness assure the return of this cosmic cycle
> Of peace, freedom, and abundance.

Double your commitment to work for the benefit of all. This altruistic motive will insure a solid foundation, so that when abundance comes your way, as it is beginning to now, you will be in shape emotionally, spiritually, and physically to fully receive what is meant for you.

Of great benefit is to consider Gaia by contributing to the emerging planetary consciousness of wellness for the planet. Take a moment now and visualize rays of blue, healing, protective light surrounding you, your family, your tribe, all beings, and Mother Earth herself. This is what "sharing the harvest" means. The correct attitude at this time is therefore one of confidence, generosity, and love. This is the winning combination that will carry you through any obstacle that may be placed in your path. Knowing and believing this will make you fearless.

Use ritual and ceremony as part of your process to release old patterns that have plagued you in the past and created obstacles on your path. If you hear the critical coyote whispering in your ear that you don't have enough of what it takes, know that this is a lie, and that enough is less than you think. Amaze yourself—jump fully into the void with all that you are and experience the joy and satisfaction that this action generates as your energy multiplies. When you feel discomfort in the nest (or on the sofa), know that it's time to spread your wings and fly.

Know well that if you choose to not embody these suggestions given by the oracle, there is no blame; however, your old patterns of procrastination, doubt, fear, and shame would resurface, and this time of great opportunity would pass you by. This coming force is not something you can put on hold and use later; you will reap the benefits of this time by moving into the light that illuminates the way, the Tao, the road less traveled. Who you roll with at this opportune time is of utmost importance, as this is not a time to go solo, but to move with and for others who match your passion and noble intent; this will increase the opportunities and focus.

Be gracious, ethical, and compassionate, and you will accomplish not only what the Tao refers to as the "Great Work," you will also bring clarity to areas formerly clouded by judgments, doubts, and fears. Know that at this juncture you are going to have help every step of the way. This is a precious time, when your guides, your inner or outer teachers and wisdom ancestors, are right at hand, lending support that will deliver you to your brand of greatness.

43. GUAI DECIDING/PARTING

Above Dui responsive, free, penetrating
Below Qian/Gan enduring Spirit power

The wisdom

Breakthrough!
No compromise.
As you part from the past
You are in a time of creative transformation.

The struggle against negativity can now come to an end. By becoming aware of this, your situation is now favored. Resist the temptation to take the path of retribution for what has been getting in the way of completion or joy, all the while remembering that our teachers often come in strange disguises, shapes, and forms. Though it may feel satisfying in the short term to strike out with words or actions against what has been holding back your progress, know that what you do now and how you behave is setting the pattern for your personal and our collective future. Karma can be a not-so-pleasant bear.

The decision to part from the past must be resolute, with no doubts and no compromise. Your benefit now is to shift frequencies.

If there are a few bad cells left behind after a cancer has been excised, the cancer will come back and grow with the vengeance of a defeated enemy that has found strength in retreat, and will kill you and your spirit, and obliterate your mission. So this is the time to speak from your heart to your tribe and loved ones, letting them know in no uncertain terms that you've decided that you'll no longer tolerate obstacles that block the way toward the greater good. Take the role of service to this ideal like a Samurai warrior defending an enlightened master; in this case, the master is your Higher Self. State your intention to eradicate all obstructions to love and harmony, and then calmly and dispassionately act on it. Write your intention down on a piece of paper and keep it in your pocket; take it out and read it during the day. State it upon arising, state it as you prepare to go to sleep. By speaking your truth, you will be garnering strength from the universe and from Spirit, and the law of attraction says you will be the attractor. Spirit will be pleased at your resolute stance in this situation, and this signaling will bring immense, clarifying energy to you.

> Resolve to overcome all obstacles.
> Eviscerate any notions that you are not deserving.
> With calmness and clear intention,
> Make your plans and execute them.

Earth is in a mode of great change. The energy for transmutation and transformation is available, more so now than ever before. If you were to act from the ego and attempt to use this energetic blast to assume control or bring injustice or harm to another, this would come back to you exponentially. You would harm yourself for sure, but more importantly you would do harm to the glimmering of a new age, the crack in the doors of perception that is opening before us all. We are moving toward a new vision of the Earth with the dawning realization of our interconnectedness. Our individual thoughts and actions are now magnified and feeding the cosmic matrix. The astrological alignments confirm this; they are mirroring these vast changes. At this potent time, negative actions will reverberate through a lifetime—this lifetime and future ones—that is how powerful these times and these energies are. So be cautious and stay awake!

Stand firm now and act decisively; you have the strength to make your battles short and focused. And be diligent in keeping your emotions out of the fray. Stay out of others' business and don't fall to the level of gossip or disrespect in your triumphs. Do not disparage your opponents in their defeat; let them be, they know not what they do, and remember, they, too, are on a learning curve. Most importantly, forgive yourself for any part you may have played in the negative dramas of the past. Do the work to leave old, negative patterns behind by bringing them into the light of awareness. Consider using ritual to banish forever the particularly gnarly mental and emotional habits that have plagued you. In this way you will rise to new heights of compassion and self-respect. From there you will attract love and abundance in ways you have desired and have previously held only in your imagination. This is a time of creative transformation, and with the proper intent you will manifest in calmness and with grace. In this way your transformation will be effortless.

Take note that Guai comes with a caveat: even in times like this, when the light is growing, darkness in the form of the ego's desire for control is likely lurking around the corner to tempt you and others. See it, recognize it for what it is, and dismiss it with prejudice. As you move forward, do not compromise your ethics or your warrior stance.

Your intuition is now at its prime and can be accessed and trusted, as it is you who will bring about the global change we are all envisioning. How so, you may ask? Speak openly of a new paradigm and live it. Take these coming days to affirm life and the shift of the ages that is happening now, headlines notwithstanding. Be of service to others with whatever you have at hand, small or large. Smile at others at work, in your community, in class, on the street, as you drive past them on life's highway, the highway of love. In this way you will lift your tribe up into the light you are seeing and feeling. By empowering others, you are, with pure intention, empowering yourself.

44. GUO COUPLING

䷫

Above Qian/Gan Heaven/energy/Spirit power
Below Sun root/tree/foundation; standing on a firm platform; wind

The wisdom The feminine returns and she is awesome;
Come to meet.
Know that she is not alone;
The ancestors are her companions.

It is proper now to go to meet the feminine, the anima, as she comes your way, embodying joy, celebration, beauty, and the gift of manifestation. This is heady stuff, and you could forget yourself and get lost in her swirl of pleasure, copulation, fertility, and the sacred. The original instructions say, "Dance with the maiden, but do not marry." Take these instructions to heart: the "she" that is presented is to embrace, not to possess, as this energy is not yours to hold onto or control.

In business, in your art, or in your personal or spiritual life, a deep encounter with the Divine Feminine is coming to you and should not be denied. It could be in the form of a sensual coupling or in a quickening that touches your heart, leading to an understanding of the shape and form of the matrix, and your place in human existence at this particular time and space. The challenge is to not go beyond your integrity as you enter into a dance with the Goddess. What she brings to you are the sacred wisdom gifts of the ancestors, which are being offered to you to use judiciously on your journey. This clean, bright energy is magnetic, intended for you to use to cleanse yourself of the darkness you may have inherited or have recently encountered. You are meant to join with this archetypal feminine energy and find a person or tribe that stimulates your mind and gets your creativity to flow like a river after a spring rain, sweet and sensual and a great, surprising pleasure to behold. You may be shifting your tribal allegiances, and if an appropriate situation presents itself, this too will be of benefit.

You have an opportunity to make real changes in the world in concert with your tribal fellows. But do not bring this mistress of strength and depth of power into your relationships—your connection is too hot and would burn any bonds you have, no matter how strong. That new personal love or the seductive opportunity on the horizon should stay there for now as you realize that this encounter with the sacred feminine is meant to be brief, and in this case brevity is what will serve you in your service to the greater good. If your encounter were not brief, you would surely be consumed.

Note that the current offer of power, riches, or sensual pleasures comes with a dark side. The ego might tell you to take all you can get to keep as your personal treasure trove, to mete out for your own aggrandizement. And it would be very tempting to do so, for power like this is rare. The ego is the quintessential trickster, making dark look like light, and vice versa. So stay in your integrity in all matters concerning the awesome power of the sacred feminine. If you don't, you will give power to the shadow side.

When you are presented with great promises—of love, position, wealth, or power—definitely go and examine the possibilities, but embrace only what works for you and dismiss the rest. This doesn't mean you will have fully moved away from the darkness; that's not the point. This hexagram is a teaching on discrimination. As you meet this energy flow halfway, honor that it has arrived, and extract only what matches your integrity. Go easy—you are literally playing with a fire that needs tending so that you are not consumed by the flames of desire and pleasure-seeking. When you dance with the darkness, you have to know when to let go and when to change partners. Look at what is on offer and accept only what works for you and leave the rest. Do not succumb to fear, but be on guard so that you are not sucked in so deep you cannot get out. Walking with integrity in the face of seduction is an important skill to acquire on the path of the spiritual warrior.

> Take note:
> The unspoken promise
> Of love, sex, easy money,
> Or quick and easy spiritual advancement
> Is a move by the troublesome, yapping coyote, the
> trickster ego.

That said, go now to meet. Keep an open mind—have encounters, examine opportunities, and join in the eternal interplay of yin and yang, but only go midway to meet. This is the jumping-in point of expanding the creative. Fate has brought you to this point, and now it's up to you to know how far to go and how deep to get in without getting burned or suffocating. Look and listen, and the truth will be revealed well before you dig yourself so far in that you are delivered to the dark forces disguised as the light. Protect yourself and honor the sacred space of ethics, compassion, and integrity.

In the present situation, any attempt to control is folly. You cannot control what the heavens bring your way. Simply let this awesome energy flow through you. Do not retreat, even if you feel afraid, as the energy of fear can actually ignite positive action.

Look deeply into your situation; it has not come about by chance. Bravely and with resolve go inward and find your still point; this will bring clarity and light into what was held in darkness. Above all, do not turn away. Face your fears, and the darkness will incrementally give way to the light. Your weaknesses will become your strengths, and your tears will give way to joy. Grieve for what or whom you must let now go of, and make your move. Steel yourself, for you will be challenged. Make any obstacles on your path your fuel.

In times of change, when you find yourself in a difficult or seemingly impossible situation, look inward, for it is self-knowledge that will always extricate you and deliver you safely to the shore. Unflinchingly, look deep within and see and embrace your dark side and the emotions that come with it. These emotions are the colors with which we paint our lives. Gaia has her own hidden dark side as well—it's a darkness that gives way to the dawning of light and love. Make your fears, tears, anger, and grief your loving companions as you travel the path toward the highest good for you, your fellow beings, and our precious Earth.

45. TS'UI GATHERING TOGETHER

Above Tui lake
Below K'un Earth

The wisdom Bring hearts and minds together;
There is a great task at hand;
Join in community with love and humility.

Where are you living? What are you doing? What are your relationships? Are you in the right relation? Where is your water? Know your garden. It is time to speak your truth. Create your community. Be good to one another. And do not look outside yourself for your leader.

These are the instructions the tribal elders give us at this point in our journey of coming home to our true human selves, free of doubt and shame, as we birth the New Earth.

Look to what you have accomplished, and in stillness, without giving quarter to anything or anyone, deconstruct what got you to this point in time, alive, inspired, and engaged. Your higher wisdom self asks you to look to your thoughts and motivations, and be sincere in your assessments and actions. If you choose a path so that you will look good to others or because it might allow you to mingle with a desired group, be very cautious, as movement like this will surely lead to a wounding that would be difficult, if not impossible, to heal.

Leadership need not mean the arrival of a knight on a white horse, banners flying—though at times this kind of flash can be useful. The leadership that the oracle speaks of is that of the leader from within. Be it family, business, personal relationships, or your own spiritual journey, your role is not to create a commonality of thought and action, but to encourage strong individuality while remaining steadfast in your truth and adhering to the highest standards of integrity and compassion in working for the greater good.

> It is not to lead by issuing orders
> Or setting limits;
> Rather, lead by encouragement,
> Working together for
> The common good.

The teachings found in the ancient sage Sun Tzu's *The Art of War* say that the great leader does not lead from in front of the troops; nor does she or he lead from behind. The great leader leads from within. It is in this way the true and righteous power of a group, community, or relationship is actualized, and great things can be accomplished.

Achieving harmony in your work with others or in your personal relationships is now required for your spirit to flourish. This is accomplished with honesty, sincerity, and integrity. In your intimate interactions, respect these moments as sacred and ceremonial, a balance between the light and the dark, yin and yang. Honor the feminine and embolden the hero.

When people gather together it's natural that there will be conflict, which can raise issues of jealousy and the quest for control and power. Know that conflict creates energy that can be used to either positive or negative ends. It is the task of the leader, the head of the clan, to convert the energy created by conflict into a positive force that can lead all concerned to their personal and collective goals. To do this, the leader must remain calm, devoted, disciplined, and centered and move with integrity, compassion, and kindness. Keep in mind that these lessons apply not only to your outer world; they are also an awesome arsenal to have to gain clarity on your inner journey. It is in this ritual space that you expose yourself to the lies you have lived and told, and forgive yourself as you shine the light on your personal shadow. This resolves all the fears and doubts that have plagued you on your path.

A great leader is not necessarily recognized as a leader at the time. Leadership, as all great tacticians know, is often achieved invisibly, without any outward acknowledgement. By maintaining a correct attitude, the rewards of completion and satisfaction are assured for one and all.

Trust yourself now. You are the leader, the one you and your tribe and all of us have been waiting for.

46. SHENG ASCENDING

Above Kun — center of the Earth; the yin element supporting all things; responsiveness

Below Sun — root, foundation; subtle penetration, like the wind; small, steady effort

The wisdom

You are in a time of advancement.
What you have been working for is on the way.
Now simply be present.
Be mindful of where you stand.

This is your season of harvest. The harvest, in this case, consists of the ripe fruits stemming from your small, steady efforts. You have been paying attention to all the details, remaining steadfast to the principles of working for the greater good as best you can, and until now it seemed as if the fruits of your efforts have been elusive. Try as you know you must to not have expectations, it's difficult not to have them. You *have* had expectations—which you've tried your best to quiet—of how your diligence would bring about a desired outcome. In the present situation your expectations are about to be humbled by the good fortune that is coming your way.

This is an excellent time to make the moves you've been holding in check, feeling that either the timing was not right or that those with influence and authority would not be receptive. Leave all worries behind.

It has seemed that in so many ways all the work and waiting has been interminable. But that was only your analytical mind interfering with the universal law of right timing. Patience and quiet nurturing are all that's needed now, whether in your relationship to your own inner self or in your projects, relationships, or your connection with Mother Earth.

It's happening; no need to push. What you have desired *is* coming your way. Don't ask when, just trust: it is now. Trust and faith combined is a powerful engine that will propel you forward in your quest for what is right and in harmony with the natural order.

> Quiet your heart and mind.
> Allow the natural way to unfold.
> Be steady, there will be no foul and no blame;
> Progress and prosperity are assured.

All the things you've worked and wished for in life are moving forward, toward the greater good. It's as if you are exactly synchronized with the calendar of your life path. The energies of the Earth and the universe are moving in harmony with you, with your actions and desires. Your intuition is at an extremely high level. Trust it and make your well-considered moves, whether in love, work, or in the care of our planet and all her beings. Bring all together and be the giver of love and life to your tribe, your family, and all your relationships.

Note well that while you may harvest the bounty that is available to you now, the benefit will be to return this energy in equal measure to the living organism of Gaia, to which you are deeply rooted. This is your family, which has silently and elegantly supported and nurtured you so that you could get to this point of beneficial harvest. Keep feeding the whole, the oneness of which each of us is a part.

Have confidence that you have done your work to this point,

that you have correctly nurtured yourself, your relationships, your tribe, your projects. Have faith that your growth is assured if you allow everything to unfold without judgment or the interference of the critical, analytical mind. Refrain from picking things apart and just let the mind relax in its own vast, natural spaciousness.

This hexagram signals that your personal magic could not be at a higher and more powerful point. Your ideas will be well-received by those around you. You will advance in your relationships and in your career, and your words will be heard. You are part of a network that is connecting all good things for the benefit of yourself, your tribe, and the world.

Stay steady and remain humble. Meditate and take part in activities that keep you centered and grounded. By adhering to the higher laws and acting with compassion, kindness, and integrity, what you will gain will remain, and any doubts about yourself will wash away like dust after a longed-for rain.

Listen to the wind as it speaks to you, hear the waters as they nurture and teach you, celebrate fire as it burns away the dross, taste of the Earth herself as she nurtures all sentient beings, and wear the air on your skin like a royal robe of ritual and celebration.

47. KUN CONFINEMENT

䷮

Above Dui — open, responsive; free movement with no blame or judgment

Below Kan — gorge, precipice, water; moving without hindrance; radiant clarity

The wisdom

Being diligent on your path
While listening intently for the seeds of truth
Has exhausted you.
You are in a state of confinement.
Words will not set you free.

Trust no one who is attempting to sway you with words of praise or offers of precisely what it is you have wanted and dreamed of. There has been a breakdown in the code, the code within language. You have expended great effort to communicate clearly and to purify your intentions and tap into your intuition. The work has been good, but now you're at your limit and you must stand down. If you were to proceed in your present state of mental and emotional exhaustion you would not only be confined as you are now, you would be caught in a trap that even time itself would not release you from for a long time.

In the preceding teachings of the I Ching there has been great credence placed on being in your truth in your communications with your tribe and associates and in your relationships. This was good, even sage advice for the time. But times have changed, as they do. A cycle that has been difficult, yet one that has contained many benefits, has come to an end. That cycle had called on you to be honest, forthright, and to communicate with clarity so that you could move toward and achieve your goals for yourself and for the greater good.

Now, in this current period of confinement, faced with the weight of adversity, you feel you *should* have the ability, because of your attention to the process, to speak all the right words that would embody your ideas, and that *should,* in a perfect world, carry you to the next stage of development and set you free. But as a cycle ends, your words are either not heard or ignored. If they are heard, they are misconstrued, and to others they take on the opposite meaning of what you intend. If you were to proceed now using your words to pave the way you would surely hit obstacle after obstacle, and the state of mental and emotional exhaustion you are in could manifest as a physical breakdown.

> Your life force feels bottled up.
> Somehow it must be released.
> Help will not come from the outside;
> Look inward for the sustenance needed to continue.

In dealing with this turning point, there is much to consider in so many aspects of your life. Some areas appear to be doing well, yet others seem dry, confined, and hopeless. Kun has appeared now because of difficulties that have in the past caused you to despair and become depressed. This is where the message of this hexagram is of great assistance. Know that this situation, which is omnipresent, is temporary, and that the assistance needed to regain the proper life flow that will replenish you emotionally, spiritually, and physically is within reach; it is, in fact, within you. The only way that relief will find you is for you to take time to rest, recreate, breathe, and remain positive, knowing that this is the end of an exhausting cycle and the beginning of a new, enlivened, exciting one; in fact, it is a renewal of life and the life force.

Your truth will be made evident not by your words, but by your actions. It is a great frustration when your words are not heard and the words you hear from others cannot be trusted on face value. These are challenging times, and you must regain your strength and call to mind your sense of purpose. The way to gain strength and release your, chi, your life force, is to undertake a plan of rest and recuperation. Plan this time of regrouping as you would plan a battle—well-thought-out and organized. Leave no place open where you could be caught unawares. Once this commitment is made, all will begin to fall into place, and recovery, creativity, and eventual success will follow.

Rest, in this situation, might mean a literal resting time, or it could simply be a retreat from trying to fix what is seemingly going wrong, trying to change people's minds or make an old way of thinking work for you. The current cycle is swiftly changing; be assured that the light needed to remove oppression and to recuperate from exhaustion is coming your way. Do not let this period of confinement piss you off and cause you to become cynical or strike out in anger. If you take that road, all will be lost, and you will not be able to benefit from the teaching given to you by Spirit in your present situation.

In fact, you will reap positive results from being in voluntary confinement while experiencing oppression. You must and will change your way of handling obstacles and old, tired ways of thinking and acting. In repose your creativity will gestate new ideas, and you will begin to hear, understand, and learn to speak the code of a new language that will emerge in the coming cycle. This will put you at the forefront, at the head of the class, while others remain in their struggle, conflict, and drama.

In this cycle, wordless actions will be of great benefit. You will learn when not to speak, and to hear beyond words to the underlying truth held in the unspoken code. This is a lesson in understanding that unlocks the mysteries of the universe that have been held in secret by priests, shamans, and sages for eons. As we awaken, individually and collectively, we will change our way of thinking, speaking, and listening. In these extraordinary times you will have an opportunity to access help from unexpected places. You will leave old, stale relationships behind as you move forward in your understanding of your sense of purpose to form new, positive associations. Look deep within yourself. There you will find the strength needed to continue.

If you feel in the days ahead a broken or troubled heart, embrace those feelings and stay steady; suffering will give way to greatness and joy. It is the Way.

48. CHING THE WELL

䷯

Above K'an water
Below Sun wind

The wisdom

Your life and your environment
Change constantly;
What does not change
Is the Source.

The well represents the holding place of nourishment for the soul, the inexhaustible source of the water of life, the source of our inner truth. It is born of the collective truth of humanity and receives from each person's life experience. In this hexagram you are being directed to go to the well and draw from the subterranean flow of the Way. Now is the time to tend to the well. What makes it strong is how you nourish yourself on a daily basis.

Your spiritual life, your inner life, requires daily attention. Tending to your spiritual life doesn't come from books or from gurus and teachers; it comes from your inner work, your daily practice, from how you live your life. Ching has come at this time to notify you that it is of utmost importance that you go deeper into your truth than ever before. If you refuse this call, then you cannot access the well, the container of nutrients needed to sustain life and foster growth, peace, and tranquility.

To supply pure, untainted water that feeds your soul and spirit, the well must be clean. Be sure that what you're taking in—spiritually, mentally, physically—is pure in truth and content. This refers to who you roll with and who you share your intimate moments with, as well as your own thoughts and worldly actions. The eye of the universe is always open, always ready to assist and equally ready to serve up lessons when you drift away from the road less traveled, the path to enlightenment. Enlightenment involves remembering who you truly are. With no judgment or fear, delve into the essence of you, the you that is untainted by family, school, religion, and social conditioning.

Ching puts you on notice that it is your responsibility to nurture not only yourself, but those around you who do not have the resources—spiritual, mental, and material—that you have been blessed with. Give back to your friends, mates, tribe, and community. Nourishing others feeds the soul and refines your nature. That is because we are all one: when a butterfly flaps its wings, a wind blows in faraway lands.

> Go to the well and be joyous.
> Make strong the well.
> Nourish the mind with quietness;
> Nourish the soul with generosity.
> Go deeper, love deeper.
> Dance the dance of life.

You have been diligent and have come to an honest place within yourself. You have effected positive changes. This is good. Recognize your accomplishments on your journey of conscious evolution, but do not get lost in self-congratulation—this is not the time. You only need to know that it is through your diligent work that you have increased your deep inner resources. You can now tap into these resources at will, to literally shape reality and bring a change of consciousness to this Earth, the change we all want and need. Ching is instructing you to use the abundant, deep resources of your body, mind, and spirit to make your community, our world, and the Earth a better place. This is your personal responsibility, and have no doubt about it, it can and will be accomplished.

Equally important, while driving down the road toward your goals you might occasionally lose sight of the importance of consciously nurturing yourself. Ching has come along to remind you to attend to the well. Call on your intuition and creativity to attend to your personal practice, your time of contemplation and quietude. Look to your daily life and see the rituals you have in place. It may be that cup of tea or coffee in the morning or the desire to sit in silence by a fire on a chilly night. Look to what you do when you leave your home in the morning or when you return. These are rituals; if you see them as ceremonies of life and treat them accordingly, with great care and respect, they will nurture your soul. By honoring your life this way, you give meaning and depth to yourself and your path.

Make time to delve into your inner thoughts, hopes, and desires, and honor and feed them. This will bring forth the love and compassion that you can give to yourself, and from there you can give the same to others. In so doing you will be a bright beacon to all those around you.

In these momentous times, with all that we are facing in our world, it is imperative that we give rise to thoughts and actions that will make the world a better place. Look to the volume of what goes into the literal and metaphorical trash bin of life on any given day, and do your share to lessen the amount. Listen to the words of the elders in your tribe or community; teach young people and those less fortunate the skills that you know. And consciously take good care of yourself, on all levels.

Strive to make the instructions contained in this hexagram,

Ching, part of your daily practice. We all have an inner voice, a Higher Self, a guide that shows us the way. Listen for and trust this voice.

Play, dance, sing, cry, and laugh—all of it feeds your soul.

49. GE SKINNING/REVOLUTION

䷰

Above Dui	open, responsive, free
Below Li	radiant, articulate
The wisdom	Strip away the old skin. Make way for Revolution.

Great change lies before you. Old ways and apathy are to be stripped away, skinned. This hexagram, Ge, recalls previous times when beings were threatened with extinction and had to innovate or die. Momentous times present great opportunities for evolution.

In the center of the field of life imagine a pond of pure, nourishing water that will fertilize the ground so that new ideas and directions will emerge to benefit all sentient beings. Go to this pond of truth; it will nourish you in this time of revolution. As in all times of dramatic change it is important to be awake and not throw the baby out with the bathwater. Be a seed saver, and separate what is of no use from the old cycle from what will be useful to plant in the coming cycle.

This is a time of molting and replenishing. Peeling away an old skin can be painful, yet through that process the truth of what will benefit you and others and what must be relegated to the compost heap will be revealed. The oracle's advice is to make your movements slow and steady. There is a need to stand firm and not rush the process; there is time to do what must be done.

The forces of conflict in the situation at hand are mirroring an inner conflict brewing just below the surface, asking you: *Are you on the right path and tending the correct garden?* Like a Zen koan, this paradoxical question has no answer, yet in contemplation you will find that it contains all answers. Drawing this hexagram signifies it is a time of revolution in your world and on your path. To be a successful revolutionary you must be strategic and have a plan. Look to the core of your actions and beliefs and assess what and how this revolutionary action will come into play.

Times such as these are often uncomfortable or painful, which in itself can pave the way for change. Consider your actions from a place of stillness and maintain your dignity and humility. In times of revolution, any display of hubris will not shield you from pain; it will only make you vulnerable to attack and take you off the road less traveled, the road that leads to self-awareness.

> Enter now the initiation.
> A new way of thinking and being will be made clear.
> Warning:
> This initiation could be uncomfortable;
> It will reveal the greatness of what lies before you.

The world is no longer the way you once knew it. Among the obstacles to knowing your truth are those who have attempted to persuade you to adopt *their* ways and *their* standards in order to fulfill *their* dreams and desires. They relish control over you and lay claim to your dreams of freedom, creativity, and wholeness. The time has come, however, for you to reclaim the essence of you and your mission and your desire to be free.

The base elements of this hexagram are metal and fire. The metal is molten by the action of fire; it represents the cycle that is transforming to create a new form that will activate a clear, creative, beneficial force in your life. The symbolism of this hexagram, Ge, tells us in no uncertain terms that you are entering, along with the rest of humanity, a new era. This is not by choice, but the result of a rich destiny that is impacting all of us now.

Timing is of the essence. To know the right time to make the necessary changes, go into stillness and trust the inner voice of wisdom. Trust that you will be guided by your intuition, which will illuminate the right time and place to shed your skin, like a glorious serpent of light giving way to its metamorphosis. Delve deep into your practice as a signal to Spirit that you are present and willing to receive assistance from your guides.

Be strategic as you look to old, worn-out modes of thinking and acting. Deconstruct your fears to see what has been generated by shame, fear, and doubt. In holding firm to your intention to transform, be utterly fearless. Literally change the words you think, words that have kept you believing you weren't good enough for the initiation into an expanded creative consciousness and an expanded self. Words and language are a code that reach into the sanctum sanctorum of your soul and manifest as realities. This is why the words you think are more powerful than the words you speak, as your thoughts create your reality.

As your old skin is being stripped away, don't look for comfort by giving up your ideals or compromising your truth. Be steadfast, compassionate, and kind as you grow a new beautiful, luminescent skin that will feel like a warm, fragrant cloak you will wear as you travel the path of awakening.

You don't have to go this alone. What's moving through you is also moving through your tribe and community, indeed, through the entire world. So invite those you hold dear to be present as your trusted witnesses, and be an inspiration for your fellow pilgrims. Speak your truth of where you are at in the dance, and take partners. You will be heartened as to how many in your circle are in the same dance. It's a new form of collaboration, and it is joyful.

50. DING — THE SACRED VESSEL

䷱

Above Li — radiance
Below Sun — the root, the base on which all things rest

The wisdom

The cauldron sits on a fire.
In the cauldron are all your ways and means.
Tend the fire carefully
Lest you overcook the brew of transformation.

The heat you are feeling is coming from deep within your consciousness. Heat is generated when initiation is at hand. As Ding is called, you are told that you have done well, and you now have a grand opportunity before you—the opportunity to make an alchemical elixir of love, spirit, and fate that if used judiciously will guide you to the gates that open to a world of peace and abundance.

You have called for this sacred vessel to be placed before you. You are to deposit your doubts and fears in the cauldron, where they will be cooked by the fire of your Higher Self, their energy thereby transforming into something useful. This boiling brew of primal metamorphosis is meant to purify your heart. From this place, all is possible; you need only take a leap of faith and accept that no matter what happens, it is the right thing at the right time. Having chosen the initiatory path, you will open your vessel to receiving guidance from Spirit. Spirit in turn will open the crystal prism of your inner vision so that you can attune to the higher frequencies and bring everything into harmonious alignment with your Higher Self.

The infinite aspects of your being
Are feeding the fire that heats the sacred vessel.
You are brewing your own transformation,
An alchemical elixir of inner knowing and understanding
Of what this journey holds for us all.

The Western mind, mired in materialism as it is, gives no credence to the idea that being in harmony with the flow of cosmic energies is necessary for advancement. Moreover, the concept of ritual sacrifice and accepting what is fated is difficult for the Western mind to wrap its head around. But nothing less than sacrifice is what's being called for at this time—you have called it forth from your very essence. Call on your warrior spirit, and with a peaceful mind and pure heart, abandon what no longer serves you. Through this act of intent you will be transformed, and your personal transformation will feed our collective transformation, and in this way will the New Earth be born. This is a game of cosmic tag, and you're it! In truth you always were it, but because of the mask you were wearing, a mask hardened by the mind control mechanisms of the state, the educational system, religious institutions, and media, you didn't know it. But now you do.

Ding, the Sacred Vessel, is bringing your destiny to the forefront of your consciousness. Societal programming has told us that fate is a negative, a limitation, a "less than." Nothing could be further from the truth. Your fate—your path and purpose—is what is to be revealed to you through this act of ritual sacrifice. This initiation will lead to renewal, to a new way of being and of being seen, as you connect with your sacred essence, the presence of the Divine. Your life then becomes art, and you are appreciated in a new and very real way. It may well be through your creative, artistic expression that you are seen, or it could be as a leader in your community, family, or tribe.

Harmonizing with the cosmos, a big concept, is, in essence, the simplest and least effortful way forward. Begin by making a change in the way you live each day. Go with joy, in harmony with nature, with Gaia, and be a blessed part in fulfilling the needs of the planet and human society. Become aware of, and fully present to, the flow of energy in your tribe, family, and personal relationships. Do not isolate at this time. You need to see and be seen, to reflect yourself and be a mirror for others in your tribe who are with you, knowingly or not, in this great transformative leap taking place on Earth at this time. You will surely have to sacrifice old programming around limitation and control, and patterns of insisting that you're right and others are wrong. Dissolve your ties to relationships that are burdens and that have kept you from your truth. Through these actions you will become inspired and be a light of hope for others to see and feel.

Ding is calling on you to examine your thoughts and the clever ways you unconsciously manipulate your own thought processes and the thinking of those around you. To follow this call, explore how your ego takes control, since the mind is the ego's favorite tool. Investigate whether you have accepted certain harsh, dogmatic beliefs or behavior as the norm, whether in your relationships, business, your craft, or in the world at large. Look carefully to see if you are harboring stale, hidebound ideas about how those in friendship or relationship with you should behave. Then make a sacrifice to Ding, the cauldron of initiation, of your critical, judgmental views, which you have defended in order to maintain the illusion of superiority and control.

Now is the time to prepare for personal transformation as the Earth, hit by higher cosmic frequencies, undergoes a gigantic leap in consciousness. Amidst the seeming chaos, the possibilities of a new era are presenting themselves, and you have invited this change—*we* have invited this change, collectively. Ding is the answer to our call.

As you travel your path, you will encounter real-life gatekeepers who keep you from your solace and inner truth. These ogres and obstacles can come in the form of people who have gained power or influence over you and who for their own ego survival do not want to let you go. Or they may come in the form of a familiar old depression or free-floating anxiety laced with doubts and fears. Ding tells you it's your job to recognize these things as gatekeepers; you must face them and not run away from them. Use the tools that have brought you to your inner truth as you have walked your walk, and confront the obstructions head-on. Your power to do so will come by moving with grace and integrity, compassion and kindness, and ruthless honesty.

Walk in nature, plant a garden, learn something new, and go deeper into your spiritual practice. Meditate, laugh, and play with the rainbow children who are all around us now as we make this Earth shift through our collective human will.

51. ZHEN THE ROUSING

Above Zhen shake, arouse, thunder, inspiration, laughter
Below Zhen shake, arouse, thunder, inspiration, laughter

The wisdom

Thunder shakes the roof;
You go back to sleep.
Big thunder comes again;
This time you are awake.

A powerful time has arrived and is manifesting as a great shaking and arousal. Your senses are turned on and keen. You feel torn between excitement and fear. Here you must choose what the benefit will be. Do you let fear cause you to back away from opportunity, letting the thunder pass as you pull the covers up over your head, wishing you didn't have to choose? Or do you risk it all and jump into the unknown?

Disappointments, losses, or catastrophes are informing you that this is a time of awakening, and once awakened you are jolted into clear consciousness, fully awake, so awake and clear that you may find it difficult to trust your intuition as to what's on the horizon. You've been disturbed and shaken to the core by recent events and difficult decisions you've made. You can't avoid this shake-up, as you are now stripped bare of your long-trusted shields that have been your protection against change, creativity, and love. The universe is speaking loudly to you to drop your chattering, analytical mind and move into your emotional and spiritual core. This can be scary.

Fear is natural when something is wrong, yet it can be an impetus to change and greater honesty and awareness. You will find clarity only when you stop lying to yourself and to those around you. In this case your lies are in your silence, in not speaking up for what is for the greater good—good for you, your community, and the Earth. Were you to ignore the thunder and go back to sleep you would wake up in a world that you definitely do not want.

Think back to the silent inner dialogue you've been having with yourself since you started your journey, the unspoken words that begin with pleas to Spirit: *I want … I wish … If only …* These are calls to spirit helpers. The shaking and shock you feel is the thunderous power of manifestation, your power of manifestation. It may come as a surprise that you've really done it this time; you've called for change, and now here it is.

> You are the magus, the creative magician.
> This shake-up is in the perfect order of things;
> It would not have come to you if you were not ready.

The process now is one of deep self-examination to come to your truth. You will not find who you are in another person, in your job, or in your art, nor will a teacher or a book define you—although the people and events in your life are always reflecting something important back to you about yourself. Deconstruct your life and those people in it to find out who you are and who you aren't. Look to all your relationships and be honest with yourself, unsparingly honest, as you look in the mirror. Ask to see all the unresolved issues that get in your way, the triggers that point to your unconscious shadow self. You will question yourself, but persevere in this process, which is the strategy of the spiritual warrior. Remain composed and aware as this virtual thunderbolt hits you, and guide its strength toward the greater good—for yourself, for your tribe and fellow pilgrims, for the Earth. It may be lonely at times, but the loneliness will transform into oneness with Spirit.

Use this time to hone your character, removing the big obstacles as well as the little flaws and wrinkles that you think no one else sees. Through the unexpected strength of recent challenging events you are being tempered and made strong. Stay in your center. When fear arises, know that due to your commitment to personal growth and change you are capable of facing fear head-on. No guarantee that you won't get a bit burned in the fray, but this is part of the agreement; the burn is from the fire of transformation, and the salve is found in stillness. Make it a practice to listen to the inner voice of wisdom, your Higher Self, every day. Once you embrace the simplicity of higher consciousness you will be able to accept with ease the great transformation that is shaking you, and you will know that this is part and parcel of the contract you made with yourself and with Spirit when you chose to incarnate at this magnificent moment in time.

Respect yourself throughout this process, and be clear, kind, and compassionate—beginning with yourself and extending that to all others. The rewards are greater than great as you flow with the collective movement toward the greater good that is the divine plan now unfolding on Planet Earth. The world is watching, seeking, longing for the light. Be the light. Teach peace and be the love you desire. You will be met in kind, no doubt about it. As the elders have taught: We are the ones we've been waiting for.

52. GEN BOUND/COMING TO STILLNESS

Above Gen mountain
Below Gen mountain

The wisdom

What was destined has become reality.
Consequences of past actions are now.
No longer consider the future;
Be here now.

Much energy has been expended to put your thoughts, ideas, and creative force into action. Now it is time for renewal in its simplest form: by coming to stillness. Look inward in meditation and contemplation.

Reflect on recent events. When a passing cycle and an approaching cycle overlap, there is often some confusion. It is in stillness that you will dispel the unease, and questions and inner turmoil will be sorted out. The benefit now is to embody the Taoist concept of w*u wei,* the action of nonaction. There is great strength to be found in *wu wei,* "effortless action." It means being at peace even while engaged in activity, a state of profound concentration and flow sometimes described as being "in the zone." In this space you do not rush around or aggressively overthink or make any attempts to control a situation; instead you're like the bamboo that bends in the wind, aligning with the benign movement of the natural world. You put your ego-driven needs aside and flow with the current, not against it.

Nondoing does not mean stop. Consider the mountain, which at first glance appears quiet and steady. But stirring beneath its surface are the activities of vast natural systems, which arise from deep within the mountain and flow outward. These are the pure waters that feed the natural cycle of birth, growth, death, and rebirth. This is you, if you choose to remain in stillness, being mindful of the depths of your being—mindful that what you think is more important than what you do. Our thoughts, words, and our very physicality are in essence vibration and frequencies. By being in inner stillness regardless of your surroundings, you can effortlessly raise the consciousness of yourself, your tribe, and your community. This action of nonaction in turn raises the vibration of the collective and Earth herself.

The Chinese ideograms that form Gen are of two mountains bound together. This denotes the end of a cycle, and during this ending you must set boundaries. By enacting boundaries, you are giving way to new choices, ideas, poetry, songs, creativity, and to new companions of destiny. In stillness, binding together as two mountains side by side, you will activate your stability. Many people and Earth herself will experience upheaval during this time, but do not fear—chaos is in the natural order when an old cycle ends and things are getting shaken up. In some it will cause great inner turmoil, as many people have long-suppressed, latent longings and shadow material that is surfacing now in rage and conflict. Remove yourself from these lower vibrations, both physically and mentally. Inwardly correct any negative self-talk that is a remnant of past experiences. Be as pure as possible in what you take in as nourishment and in your thoughts and words.

Reaffirm your boundaries.
Be inwardly still and calm.
Adhere to the Tao of nondoing.
There you will find your strength.

Join with your fellow pilgrims on your soul's journey to enlightenment, and freely talk about what you are feeling as the great turning unfolds. Break the ice in conversations, and you will be delighted and surprised that your thinking is not weird or New Age claptrap—it is stirring in all of us now. Make your home and table a salon of interesting new people with new ideas, people who are not afraid of what the changes will bring. Gather together and share what you see and feel as all bind together in clarity and love.

Earth is populated with amazing beings who have been incarnating for many centuries, waiting for this momentous time. You may, without consciously knowing it, be one of these beings yourself. Pay attention to the elders who are coming to the forefront with their teachings, which are attuned to the incoming galactic energy waves. This is why we must cultivate stillness, so we can hear their messages. How do you differentiate true teachings from ego-trapping messages that have programmed you up to now? Simple: use your body as a barometer. You will feel what is true and right somatically, and it will feel good; what is not true will not. This simplicity is what makes it powerful. Trust your body, the container of your soul and Higher Self—it will never lead you astray.

Meditate in your own way, a form you've learned and practiced, or simply go to a place of peace within, or to an actual place where you find great peace. This is not something to do later, when you have the time. The time is *now!* Set the bar high, be an example, a beacon for all to feel and see. In your stillness you will teach; in your stillness you will learn; in your stillness you will be found.

53. JIAN GRADUAL ADVANCE

䷴

Above Sun — root, foundation, wood; standing on a firm foundation; nourishing penetration; slow

Below Gen — quiet mountain; unshakable, steady, firm, and still

The wisdom

Situations and relationships
Are in the developing stage;
Move carefully and observe tradition.

Time seems to be moving at a near-unbelievable speed. In a blink of an eye, it seems, the year is over. Months feel like a week, and a week but a day. Do not get swept up in this energetic push into the unknown, which is the illusion of linear time. If your movements were to try to match this fantastical speed you would become exhausted—*are* exhausted. Trying to keep up with unconsidered actions or attempting to gain control of the situation at hand, you would miss what is beneficial when presented with a challenge such as this. Building a structure of any kind at an ill-considered speed would result in a weak and fragile state of affairs. The benefit now is to find stillness in the midst of chaos, and from this state of being you will achieve something strong, long-lasting, and secure.

By moving slowly and deliberately, the changes and enhancements to your life, which you are just getting a hint of, will come into the light of your truth and will manifest as abundance in this coming cycle. Look calmly and with a loving and nonjudgmental heart as you see and feel what is moving toward you, and then let it be; don't tinker with it, and do not doubt that destiny is in alignment now.

The new and longed-for cycle is here, and it is grand. The seeds have been planted. You have set things in order to bring this about. Appreciate it and let the timing unfold naturally. Don't lose heart because it looks like things are moving at a glacial pace—and definitely don't push. Among other lessons, this is a test of your patience and perseverance. Attend to the small details of life, bringing them to completion; this is necessary to clear the decks and to calm the mind.

Change has been manifesting all around you and through you recently, and it is change on a grand scale. But this change is not like the flip of a coin, moving instantly from black to white or from yin to yang; it will be gradual and steady. It will imbue you with lasting strength and tempered power. Whether your situation concerns a relationship, health, business, a creative project, or your spiritual path, or if the object of your concern is the world at large, in all cases allowing things to develop slowly and steadily, paying attention to the small things of life, will provide you with the spaciousness you need to develop insight into your soul's journey.

> What will be great
> Like the mountain,
> Develops slowly.

Move with purity of intent into a trusting, meditative space, one of peace and tranquility. This will allow you to receive what you, in your higher wisdom, have not only desired, but have earned within a very honorable cycle, one that has been laced with suffering, suffering that will become the gateway to exultation.

The restless ego might tell you that things are developing too slowly, *so you'd better speed up and make things happen!* But following the ego's urgings would be dangerous—you would be doing and controlling, making effort rather than receiving and allowing grace to unfold in due course. By relaxing into the flow of events as they naturally occur and not resisting or pushing, you will find the tranquility that leads to supreme success. Moreover, moving steadily at a well-considered pace will be more effective than if you were to completely stop, for if out of fear or doubt you were to stop, much would be lost, and the abundance and success that would come as a result of remaining in a receptive position would pass.

In this part of the cycle you may feel like you don't have the strength or energetic reserves to handle the massive shift that you know is coming. Don't worry—this lesson from ancestral wisdom comes in time to let you know that the correct action during this cycle is to move slowly and gracefully, with the energy of the feminine, surrounding and encompassing. In this way you will tap into hidden reserves of strength that are otherwise not available. We are set up this way; this is the way to the profound inner resources that are possessed by human beings when they are in touch with their divine presence. It's the natural way. Renew the purity of your intent for the greater good at this very important juncture of time, thought, spirit, feeling, and space. This is the perfect time to serve Gaia by simply being.

This hexagram, Jian, is a revelation of the universal laws that can be applied to business, creative endeavors, health, and to the compassionate release of old, dangerous associations and ancestral patterns that when transformed or discarded will pave the way to a tranquil place within. Jian is a window into the true essence of life, where love, peace, happiness, abundance, and acceptance in the vast, interconnected whole reside.

This time is a gift. Be grateful and gracious and accept these blessings with humility. In so doing, you will move beyond any anxiety, doubts, or fears, as you have nothing to lose, and you will actually enjoy this time of gradual progress toward your soul's destiny.

The natural order of things does not push the tree to grow faster, nor does it try to influence the speed or course of the river. Set your vision and see the beauty of slow and steady progress as it gracefully unfolds to benefit you, all those around you, and the greater good. Inherent to this action is the cultivation of a peaceful mind and a kind and gentle heart.

54. GUI MEI SUBORDINATE/CONVERTING

䷵

Above Zhen — shake, excite, inspire
Below Dui — open, free, unhindered

The wisdom

There is an imbalance.
A relationship is in formation.
Do not stand out.
Shroud your greatness.

In the classic Yi Jing, this hexagram signifies a maiden who is to be married into an influential household. The wise older woman of the family advises her not to make waves and to be still, to listen and subordinate herself to the family until she has achieved a deeper level of knowledge, maturity, trust, clarity, and contemplation. Only then will she be advised to assert herself and her ideas.

Look to this metaphor as it applies to your present situation. When you work hard for a desired goal or union it would be destructive to exert your influence too soon, as the energy of dynamic change is, for the moment, blocked, out of balance.

This is not the time to express your inner truth. If you try to be the truth-talker now, your words would be construed as being negative and counterproductive—though you know they're not. Overt corrective action would cause you to lose the opportunity to join with your desired clan, person, or group. Showing your intellect, humor, or wisdom now would cast you out of the inner circle you wish to join or the heart you wish to be in harmony with. This time requires a period of maturation no matter what your chronological age or how much experience you've clocked on the trail.

It is a precarious time.
You are on the brink
Of joining with others.
For now remain still.

While holding back, this is a good time to deconstruct what in the past have been ego-based actions. These actions, if repeated, would create obstacles and would stifle your movement toward the greater good and take you off the mark of finding peace, love, and abundance.

If you look closely you will find that the situation is such that weak people with dark intentions have come into influence and are guarding their position. To show your light and your wisdom now would be seen as a threat, and you would be held from joining the family, relationship, group, or tribe you desire and who desire you. As hard a pill as it may be to swallow, be subordinate. This will allow you to see the inner workings of the situation, where many truths are currently hidden from view. If, prodded by the voice of the ego, you were to bluster your way in, you would be rebuked; truths would not be revealed, and all your hard work would be destroyed, and you would be sent back to begin anew.

This is meant to be a prosperous cycle provided you adhere to correctness by not caring what others think and ignoring the nagging voice of the ego, which wants you to move into the light of this person or that group. Now is the time to walk in stillness and humility, and not shine in any way. It takes great discipline to walk the quiet path; now is that time.

Although you have learned and experienced much in moving toward your goal, you still need to acquire a deep, mystical knowledge of the situation so that at the proper time you can step up and exert the influence that will bring the relationship, business, or community into a beneficial position. The benefit now is to wait until the bell of intuition rings and you step into the light, surprising and outshining those who denigrated or ignored you. Trust this process. Before a novitiate is welcomed into the temple she must be humble, unseen, and subservient.

So for now, metaphorically bow your head while you determine the lay of the land. Bide your time. Wait for the right moment to move. Quiet the ego, meditate, and feed the soul. Find a place of safety, where laughter and kindness are your companions. Accept that your time of influence is not yet.

Not yet does not mean never. It means that the energies are not in alignment for you to exert influence on the situation at this time. So be a part of the nameless crowd or a member of the team who works diligently and is quietly of service. It is from this position behind the scenes that you will observe where there are dangers and pitfalls. Become a secret agent of the soul, so that when you make your move into the inner sanctum of your desired position you will do so with ease, style, and grace. This will be the dance you have desired, the dance of love, which nourishes life.

Be aware that the elders are observing you as you adapt to the morays of the situation. You will soon be recognized for your value and will have their support and blessings. Meanwhile, at this time be without visible direction; it is the direction of no direction that will lead to the harvest. To attain your desired goal, be correct in your speech and actions.

You need not feel lonely on the quiet path; your ancestors of spirit are with you and are pleased. As you walk alone, sing every day. Your voice will please spirit. Sing with no judgment of good or bad, just be fully in your song.

55. FENG ABUNDANCE/FULLNESS

䷶

Above Chen — the arousing, thunder
Below Li — the clinging, flame

The wisdom

You are in the space between lightning
and thunder,
The image of abundance.
Gather the beauty that surrounds you;
You are empowered to spread joy and fairness.

The flame in this hexagram represents clarity. Thunder indicates movement. Here we are given to look at the current situation, the timing being presented to us. We are asked to examine it carefully in the light of clarity. When we lift the veil that keeps us from being in full awareness, we see that we are indeed in a time of increase, a time of abundance.

Abundance can be fleeting; it may have the volume of a mountain or be as small as a seed. We are asked to recognize the mountain and to gather the seeds. Honor them, empower them, and let them, in their own sweet time, grow into their, and your, destiny, knowing that this timing shall pass.

Recognizing abundance brings success.
Your wisdom knows it is fleeting.
Do not dwell on this;
Be here now to quietly shine like the midday sun.

In all aspects of life there are to be found seeds of abundance, the seeds of fullness, humor, satisfaction, and joy. Consider that at this time you are an archeologist of the soul, excavating those seeds that will feed your movement through both good times and bad.

Abundance means greatness. When you find greatness you are advised to share it, to spread light and happiness to all your relationships. This is the only way to maintain it so that it does not diminish. If you try to hide your fullness, your greatness, keeping it all to yourself, abundance will surely leave, and you will be sad. But by shining and spreading seeds of joy you will join with a force greater than great. This infinite source of light feeds and fuels all living things. This has been confirmed by mathematics and physics.

Nothing remains the same. Nothing remains static. The I Ching speaks of opposites and opportunities. When you are in a time of fullness—some might call it luck—you sense that it will pass and that you must make the most of it. If you are in a time of decrease, you must look deep into your situation and find what's working and know that the seeds of increase are present there, too.

Having received this hexagram, Feng, you are put on notice that you have a window of opportunity to make your place in the world fuller and more joyous, thus ensuring a bright and loving future. Do not let this opportunity, this timing, pass, for it may not come again for a long time. Carpe diem!

When our world, our society, and our governments are in a time of darkness, it takes extra effort to find what is good, the light that feeds your soul. When you go on this adventure of discovery you are lighting your proverbial candle, which joins with all the other heart flames to bring light into the world, and most importantly, to one another.

I have a great friend who, when during his day he encounters a friend, a worker, a waiter or waitress, a shopkeeper, or a human being on the street who looks lost or is enveloped in sadness, he smiles and engages them and inquires with genuine interest on how they're doing in that moment. It always works. They are changed. They smile because their flame is recognized.

Carry your abundance, your greatness, with you. Do as my friend does and plant those seeds of caring and fullness. In this action you will dispense your magic and make the world a better place. Can anyone ask for more?

56. LU THE WANDERER

䷷

Above Li fire
Below Ken mountain

The wisdom

Passion.
Disassociate from complacency;
The wanderer comes home.

All share the desire for safety and to feel secure in work, love, and on the journey to expanded awareness. At this point in our planetary evolution take a moment to reflect on your efforts to accomplish security and peace of mind. It looks from the outside that you have done well, yet in your depths you do not feel this way. You are spurred by the fire burning in your heart; it is the fire of passion, and the work now is to recognize it and allow it to take you to new heights. Herein lies the question: What *is* my passion?

Dissatisfaction can feel disturbing, yet it is a needed impetus that challenges you to deepen your knowledge of yourself and to find the truth of who you are and why you have incarnated at this precarious moment in time.

This hexagram contains a two-part message: Take time to look at the truth your inner wisdom has been bringing to the forefront. And with this knowledge you are being challenged to move into the unknown, the unfamiliar.

While the outer view looks good and indicates that you are free, when you move to the inner journey you will find, through honest and sometimes brutal self-assessment, that there are many places where you have bartered your own truth for safety, place, or gain.

This is imprisonment, and likely along with it you have shielded your heart from being fully capable of giving and receiving love.

When risk is inevitable, we inevitably try to assess which move is the least risky. However, at this point in your personal evolution it's not about choosing the least dangerous risk, as the hexagram Lu is challenging you to take the most risky path. This is the road of the spiritual warrior, where you recognize the heat burning within, causing your mind and heart to race. Move off your position of safety and complacency and take the leap, no matter how dangerous it may seem.

You are in your comfort zone;
You know something is missing;
The missing piece
Is waiting for you,
Concealed in the unknown.

Going on a journey of discovery is best accomplished by moving away from the familiar. It's hard to break old patterns and see things with a fresh perspective if you allow yourself to settle into the same old, familiar groove.

All the good work you have done has led to this time of the quest. The quest is an ancient tribal ritual. There is the quest to find a longed-for teacher, a sage. There is the vision quest, the quest for mindfulness, and the quest for love. If you choose to avoid the time of the quest you are doomed to remain in that dent in the sofa, repeating the old patterns that have not worked out very well.

The act of traveling is vital if you wish to arrive at the realizations that await you. Whether it's a day trip, a getaway that takes days or more, or a metaphorical trip, the important thing is that you go somewhere unfamiliar, somewhere you have never been before or do not know very well. It is in unknown territory that you can clear your mind and quiet the voice of doubt. Attitude is everything when traveling: remain modest and know that you will be moving on. Be willing to drop preconceived ideas and enter an open state of mind, which can lead you to some very real places.

On the road less traveled is where you'll be able to find the clarity that will allow you to gain knowledge of exactly what's been lacking in your life and the lie you bought into that has held you back from your bliss.

When the Wanderer appears, it signifies that you have arrived at a dynamic time of transformation. In this place you will see that what you have desired is not only within reach, it is moving toward you, just as you move toward it. At this point there is no need to strive; just make yourself still and be ready to receive. It's already there, waiting for you. What allows you to be ready to receive is contained in the instructions given in this hexagram: reach for your inner fire, your passion; and step away from the familiar so you can think more clearly and in a different way. Let go of the same old ways of doing business and being in relationships that have fed just a part of you and have not truly touched your sacred core. When you choose this journey, the ego may try to convince you that things are just fine—they're good enough. But you know in your heart of hearts they aren't good enough; you deserve more.

The journey to the inner sage is not a holiday excursion or an escape; its purpose is to call on your inner fire, your passion for life, which will supply you with all the fuel you need for the quest.

In practice, following these instructions is not difficult; it's summoning the courage to take the initial risk that's the hardest part, the first step. After that, all will fall into place, and you will be free and turned on by your passion, and will attract people and situations that meet your passion.

We need your clarity and passion for the truth now more than ever before as the world is in an epic transition. Take the risk as a warrior of consciousness and truth-telling.

57. SUN THE GENTLE

Above Sun gentle wind
Below Sun gentle wind

The wisdom The truth in your situation is hidden;
It is this truth that will remove the obstacles
And set you free.

You are confronted with obstacles. These obstacles are the attitudes and patterns that you or those around you have adopted; they have created a curtain between you and the truth of the current situation.

When we seek the power of truth, it must be understood that this cannot be done with aggression or harsh words. Instead, we must proceed like the gentle wind, penetrating slowly and persistently. *Stealth* is the watchword. As the silence of the Gentle is invoked, be steady and correct your actions, and use gentle persuasion.

To make changes in your own attitudes and patterns and in those of others, you must build trust. Trust will not be achieved by raising the sword of confrontation, control, manipulation, forcefulness, or criticism. Being correct, thoughtful, and consistent is necessary as you proceed toward success, and if you wish to be understood yourself.

You may be getting frustrated by the pace at which your associates, friends, or intimate relationships are moving. Soften and bend with the situation. Do not confuse gentleness with weakness, for it is not that. You are simply adapting to the momentum of others, but with an attitude of correctness as you gently proceed toward your desired outcome.

> As a steady, gentle wind
> Bends a tree to its form,
> So will gentle persuasion soften
> The harshest attitudes.

In nature, a powerful and sudden wind can tear at the landscape, stripping trees bare or uprooting them. In dealing with our mates and business associates or with our own health matters, harsh attitudes, words, or actions can cause destruction that may take eons to repair. Take note of the lesson of the tree perched on the cliff above the sea: because it has made an artful adaptation to the wind, dancing with the wind, it has remained rooted and strong and beautiful.

This is your mission now: to be the penetrating wind of truth, compassion, and strength. In this way you will find that others will follow you in this gentle dance.

Balance is called for in your situation. First achieve balance within yourself. Renew your practice. Regular meditation, proper diet, and exercise are important if you are to remove the obstacles to your success and accomplish your goal. You must be inwardly strong to be outwardly gentle.

You will need endurance to bring your dreams, your project, or your relationship to fruition. The idea of the gentle, penetrating wind is an easy one to imagine: your influence must be consistent. You cannot let up. You must be gently persuasive. You must continue with these small acts until the obstacles disappear. Then, without anyone really noticing, the obstructions will be gone, and the light in your situation will be revealed.

This is a much more powerful tactic than using force, coerciveness, or anger. Tell no one that they're wrong; nor should you tell them that you've caught them in a lie or an act of dishonor. This will only increase and feed the negativity that created the obstacle in the first place. If you attempt to remove the obstruction or change behavior by aggressive means, it will only return later as an even bigger monster than when it first reared its head.

Your mind can be reactive, and the ego, the judge, would have you raise the proverbial sword to slash away at the obstacle before you. Do not threaten or be coercive; that is the movement of the weak and ineffective. You must temper any such impulses and instead slow down, moving at the same pace as those around you. Move slowly, persuasively, and gently. But do move—you must be alert and not stop with your attitude of gentle penetration. Just as the seasons persist, year after year, as they renew the cycle of life on Earth, so must you learn from this sage example: be persistent, enduring, and gentle.

When a young dog is being trained to relieve itself outside or on the paper, it won't work to yell at the dog when he misses or leaves a mess. Being harsh will only raise the dog's fear and anxiety and make the situation worse. The proper action is to gently but firmly put the dog outside or on the paper, over and over again, until it has learned the new behavior. This new behavior does not come about by just doing this once; it is a repeated practice. When accomplished correctly, the dog is rewarded, and thus the proper behavior becomes a good habit.

So it is in your situation: gently repeat, through words or by modeling the correct way, until the change is in place and the obstacle is removed. By being gentle, correct, and persistent, you develop trust. It is trust that brings things to continuing order and ultimately to success.

You can now create a magical situation. And as with all good magic, no one can really tell just how the result was achieved—they just know it was. It happened discreetly.

The teaching contained in Sun is to move slowly and deliberately toward the goal you desire. Be invisible like the steady, gentle wind, but never be harsh or give up. Be persistent with the strength of the steady, gentle wind. Proceed in this way and you will be loved and trusted, and in turn you will love and trust.

58. DUI THE OPEN/JOYFUL EXPRESSION

Above Dui	grow, harvest, trial
Below Dui	grow, harvest, trial

The wisdom

Spirit has been called on;
A long-closed doorway is open;
Excitement and pleasure abound;
Opportunities draw near.

As we, the tribes of Earth peoples, make ready for the shift of the ages, the feeling that we are all riding a bliss wave of eternal transformation is palpable. The gifts of body, mind, and spirit that you have withheld from yourself, your tribe, and your family are now ready to be released as new ways of thinking and being. Consciously and perhaps unconsciously you have been waiting for just the right time or hoping there would be a right time, a tribe of fellows and a place of safety to express what's been building up inside you. The fear of rejection doesn't matter anymore. It's not about how or by whom you will be received; reception lies in Spirit, not in any relationship. By moving forward without hesitation or self-judgment, you will be embraced, and in this embrace you will find the love, peace of mind, sense of purpose, and abundance you have desired. Reflect for a moment and see that through the tangle of fears and doubts you have reached a blessed clearing.

This kua, Dui, signifies that a beneficial time has arrived, a cycle of growth and good fortune, so it is not a time to sit back and do nothing. Be prepared when opportunity comes your way and move with integrity and seize the moment. Preparation, in this case, begins by accessing stillness. By contacting your Higher Self, your touchstone, you will have positive advancement in all matters.

The correct action now is to move out into the world and spread joy, bring pleasure, and share the gifts you have received from the Divine. Encourage others to join with you in a symphony of mutual loving support. This will lead to plentitude for all concerned. Work together with your choice of like-minded persons in your tribe, business, and circle of friends. Notice and point out their best qualities and attributes they may have forgotten, taken for granted, or have yet to discover. Be the teacher and teach love by being love; it is by so doing that you will be available to receive what you have long desired.

> Many opportunities are approaching.
> Some will be presented as challenges,
> Others will match your rhythm and frequency.
> You are now ready to penetrate into the heart of
> the matter—
> *Your* heart and what matters to *you*.

Mindful penetration brings action, and you are ready. It will be of benefit to proceed in concert with others in your circle and tribe. Coming now is a new relationship, project, or business opportunity that is just beginning to open; this time it wears a very different hat than what has been presented to you in the past. Open your warrior heart, the heart you have protected out of fear of discovery and rejection. Freely nurture it with basic, elemental truth, the truth that comes from your inner voice of wisdom. Be wary of getting intoxicated by this new opportunity and thrown off by the ego; be inwardly still and remain in your center.

Communication with like-minded others and with your inner creative self is enhanced now and made easy as you listen and are fully alert. Enter into the depth of conversation; this will feed you now as never before, which is why it is so important that you move *with* others, not individually. Synergy is not found in isolation or in confining your true self. Openly express your natural joy, and set your intent to accomplish great things together. Who is your community? Who is your tribe of fellows that will join you on the good road, the road of compassion and completion? Once you find your fellow travelers, you should inspire their movement, point out their talents, and be supportive. You will receive in kind. Such combining and nurturing will link minds and hearts, and in that way we will manifest what is needed at this time as we move in solidarity toward the greater good.

During this time it is by penetrating into your own resistance, which will be shown to you and will be surprisingly clear and simple to understand, that you will come to know your false self. In recognizing this you'll be able to release the old programming and the traumas of birth, family, school, church, and state that have defined you and imprisoned you. This can be a revolution in your basic psychology and physiology. You are free to share your joy and excitement about these discoveries. The aspects of your true self that have been unexpressed for so long are no longer your potential—they are your reality. These deeply held gems are rising and ready to to be revealed in glorious expressions of creativity, self-worth, and confidence.

Now is the time to encourage the sharing of ideas and theories, no matter how out of the box they may seem, and speak up when you feel or see that the truth is being concealed. Nurture shared ideas; it is in this way that the shift will happen—ecologically, financially, spiritually. We are each and every one of us clearing the way for a time when we will live together in peace, with a conscious awareness of our interdependence, caring for one another and the Earth and sharing our many blessings.

59. HUAN DISPERSION

䷺

Above	Sun	wind
Below	K'an	water

The wisdom

You are becalmed,
Motionless,
Adrift on the sea of success.
The wind is now here,
Make ready the sails.

A gentle wind is rising over the water. This indicates that the obstacles that have been blocking your progress are now calmly and gently being swept away.

There have been barriers placed before you. Odd as it may seem, we often fear our greatness, our potential for success. This is your situation: you have not fully trusted that you are capable of reaching the success you desire and dream of, so you have subconsciously put blocks in the way to give you an easy way out. This is not fear of failure; it is fear of success. The seasons have changed, however, and you now are ready to receive the instructions on how to remove the obstacles. Look to your thoughts and feelings about your associates or your relationships with intimates, family, friends, or associates. It is these nagging, judgmental thoughts and difficult emotions, fanned by the fire of the ego, that have created the obstacles to your movement forward.

Communication is the key to dispersing and letting go of petty disagreements or misunderstandings. The appearance of this hexagram, Huan, is to announce that it is now time to work in union with those around you.

Your inner guidance or perhaps a sage in your life has been speaking softly and with great clarity, guiding you back home to your inner truth. Your fear has prevented you from hearing. The gentle wind now is dispersing your fears. Set your ego aside and listen to the words of wisdom as you make your way home.

> Be calm, loving, and persistent.
> Communicate and cooperate.
> You will find you are trusted
> And loved.
> Sweet relief.

Obstacles and disappointments have been your teachers and task-masters. You see that clearly. Huan is here to tell you that you now have the strength and vision to move beyond your fear of success and of being loved for who you truly are. There has been a lack of communication and a stubbornness about asking for help, and this has kept you from dispersing the cause of disharmony that has resulted in a lack of progress.

It is time to ignite the alchemical fire that will align you with the universal laws that bring love, joy, co-creativity, and abundance. That fire is the fire of Spirit. Take time to raise the vibration of all around you. Bring your fellows together and acknowledge that the seasons have changed. Approach those you honor and who honor you. With an open heart speak of the future you see and desire. Ask for help. Be open and listen to the words that come back to you. Do not let your ego keep you from hearing.

The metaphor of the seasons clearly shows where you were and where you're headed. Winter had frozen the waters that blocked your progress. The gentle wind of spring is here and is melting the ice, allowing you to catch the wind of progress. Be gentle with yourself through this new beginning. Move slowly and with the persistence of the gentle wind blowing over the water.

In recent dealings with others you have perceived that you have not been treated well or with the respect you deserve. This may well be so, and it has caused a hardness in you. You have begun to be intractable in order to protect yourself—*I'll never let that happen to me again,* sounds the voice of the ego. This is where the danger lies. The truth is, you probably saw it coming but were so wrapped up in your own desires or your emotions that you didn't pay heed to the inner sage, the voice of the Higher Self. No blame—that was then, this is now. A new season has arrived, and the winds of change are here. You must use different methods now. Look inward, with honesty. Keep the doors of communication fully open. Make a concerted effort to transcend the things that divide you from those around you. Be calm and persistent as the gentle wind in your efforts to reunite.

This can be a time of opportunity, a time when love and abundance are available. They are knocking at your door. Let them in.

60. JIE ARTICULATING/BOUNDARIES

Above	Kan	gorge, precipice, snare; a critical time
Below	Dui	open, radiance, pause; moving freely

The wisdom

You have reached an intersection in time,
Not space.
Boundaries must be firmly stated,
Recognized, and respected.

Setting boundaries is of utmost importance at this time. Your primal self needs boundaries in order to operate in the most efficient, loving, healthy way. Without clear boundaries, all you know and love can fall into chaos, and all you have worked and cared for will hit the proverbial fan.

Whether expenditures of energy, money, or emotions, it is beneficial at this time to set limits. Not that your potential is limited—in fact, it's without limits. But the energy and effort you expend to get there does have limits that must be recognized. Your physical, spiritual, and emotional energy are sacred gifts, expressions of Spirit incarnate, and so it is a wise person who doesn't squander these gifts. To do so would be the ultimate in disrespect for yourself and for your hard-earned place living at this time on Planet Earth. By caring for yourself and ultimately for your soul's journey by setting correct boundaries, you will serve the greater good.

Knowing and honoring your limits
Brings success in great measure;
Moving outside your inner truth
Will leave you wanting and fearful.

The limits or boundaries you set must be well-thought-out. They should not be punitive or severe. Love within your present capability and plan projects that reflect where your skills and experience lie at this moment in time. Set financial limits according to your present means. Most importantly, be of service to others, but know and respect your own needs first.

Your progress will be accelerated by moving away from and letting go of those people or situations that no longer serve you and the greater good. In doing so, take an honest look inward, at who or what you might be holding in an unstated form of bondage, and quickly set them or it free. If you are unsure or fear loss, know that what is yours will return to you clean and refreshed, and will be in harmony with your soul's frequency. This is where true love and friendship reside.

To achieve optimum physical, mental, and spiritual wellness, make an honest assessment of your personal gifts and attributes as well as your limitations. The ego sometimes gives the message that if you don't move quickly and give beyond your measure, you'll miss the boat. However, the universal laws say the opposite: if you move steadily toward your goal with self-awareness, keeping your boundaries firm, when you do arrive at your destination you'll be strong and able to recognize and receive the rewards earned through the application of compassion, correctness, loving-kindness, commitment, and steady, considered effort.

The message of this kua contains the equally important instruction to set limits on limitations. Strive to not underestimate your capabilities. If that's you, recognize it as the ego's ploy to get you to play it safe, and instead break out of confining self-restriction imposed by fears and doubts. This should be done with an awareness of not going too far in the opposite extreme. Be outrageous and be courageous. Be moderate in your moderation. By all means play, love, laugh, sing, dance, and eat clean and well. Have compassion for all sentient beings, honor family and friends, and give love and support to those less fortunate than you—all within your known limits.

Body, mind, and spirit must work in harmony. You will achieve benefit by not overusing your body's resources by consuming toxic foods and chemicals. Negative thoughts and practices negatively impact the Earth's vibrational body as well as our own, so nourish your body, mind, and spirit so that you can be a good and proper caretaker of the temporary gift of your miraculous human incarnation. Similarly, you will benefit from feeding the emerging New Earth frequencies with love, the nutrient that keeps her from harm and allows all human tribes to live together on this island in space in peace and goodness. At this time it is your personal responsibility to be a caretaker of the Earth. This is simply payback for all the blessings you have received on this life path.

Dreams—both waking and sleeping—are imaginings and contain messages of possibilities. If you do not have dreams or do not honor their presence you won't know when your dreams come true, and that would be a pity as you would miss out on that joy, fulfillment, and satisfaction. As you work, live, and love within your considered limits, your dreams, on their own, without you prodding them, will manifest, as will the love and depth of feeling that you've desired. In your creative and spiritual life, as you move to express your deepest self, knowing your limitations will be as important as the medium you choose to work in. These considerations are elemental.

We are at a tipping point on this planet, and we are each a reflection of this situation and time. This hexagram contains a poignant message for your family, your tribe, and yourself. Hear the voice of Gaia—in the wind moving through the trees, in the sounds of the birds, in the rain and the moving water. Listen with your heart and your whole body, not just your mind. Honor yourself, and from there, with a loving hand, reach out to all beings. The Lakota phrase *Mitakuye Oyasin,* "All My Relations," expresses a worldview of interconnectedness and oneness that deserves our attention during these difficult times of transition.

Be the love you desire as you become a beacon of stillness and peace. Let this be your service and your teaching to your tribe and fellow pilgrims on the road less traveled.

61. CHUNG FU INNER TRUTH/INFLUENCE

䷼

Above Sun wind
Below Tui lake

The wisdom

Your heart knows the truth.
Your actions and thoughts
Must be for the benefit of all.
Limit your words;
They have little or no effect.

The wind is unseen as it stirs the waters of the lake. Invisible forces are at work to bring you success. This is a very favorable time, provided you allow the forces in your present situation to act on you.

Your situation has at times seemed untenable. You have tried to influence others with words and common sense, and it hasn't worked. You may have perceived your situation incorrectly. Go into stillness, for it is in this quiet place that the answers to your questions reside.

The upper trigram, Sun, relates to gentleness, while the lower trigram, Tui, is imbued with joy. Though it appears that certain people are blocking your progress, they will be moved toward your favor. This is assured. In the teaching offered by this hexagram you will learn how to do this gently and without words. It will be done by means of the invisible forces of gentleness and joyfulness.

To correctly influence others, you must first walk a mile in their moccasins. This will allow you to know their position and their thoughts. With this empathic knowing you can then access your intuition, which will counsel you on correct action.

Be steady and move forward with no prejudice or hidden agenda. This will create openness, which is the wordless, gentle joy of which this hexagram speaks.

> Thoughts have great influence.
> Correct thoughts free of prejudice
> Bring a bountiful outcome.
> Negative thoughts will undo
> Any good you have accomplished.

Exerting influence can be a tricky business. Thoughts and actions that attempt to manipulate or gain power over others leave nothing but animosity and resentment in their tracks and will not achieve your goals. Look to your motives in exerting influence. When you are confident that you are coming from your highest good, for the good of all, you will find that your influence, though apparently invisible, is as powerful as the wind that stirs the waters.

It seems that just when we are on the brink of success and released from bondage we are challenged as never before. It's not that you have done anything incorrectly—far from it. It is rather a law of the universe. That is the nature of the present situation. The teaching in this hexagram says to go inward and begin the task of gentle self-correction. Where it may be easy to control the words you say, it is more difficult to shift your thoughts so that they are without prejudice, divisiveness, retaliation, or anger.

There are times when we must move stubborn or obstinate people, whether in our work or in our personal lives, toward the greater good. Such an approach must be well-considered. Be gentle, with no judgment or preconceived notions. Try to understand where the other party is coming from and then adjust your thoughts, not your words, toward a more beneficial outcome for all involved. In this way your influence is directed by compassion. And having compassion for those who are slowing or blocking progress leads to a deeper understanding of oneself as well as others. This is fortunate.

Inwardly, correct any negative or judgmental thoughts. Outwardly, communicate directly and be honest and sincere. This will release your untapped life force, your prana, which in turn will have a profound beneficial effect on your relationships, your health, and your business, and will deepen your spiritual journey—all toward the greater good.

It is well-documented that we can heal many illnesses through right thoughts and meditation. You can apply this to your present situation. You are the healer. Look to the words that come to you mentally; discard the negative ones and replace them with compassionate thoughts, which will influence all those around you. In this way you will change the situation; it will move toward the highest, most beneficial good for all.

You cannot gain the trust of others until you trust yourself. This hexagram gives us a teaching on how to gain the kind of trust that comes from knowing our inner truth. Consciously look to your highest good. To be loved, you must love yourself. To be heard, you must hear yourself. To correct a situation, you must correct yourself and your inner thoughts. The outcome of this process is rich, but the process itself is even richer. This time is not about choice; it's about necessity. Love, compassion, and knowing your inner truth are what's necessary to bring about the grand success that awaits you.

So, be the wind; be the lake; be the love. And be grateful.

62. XIAO GUO SMALL MOVEMENTS/BIRD IN FLIGHT

䷽

Above	Zhen	shake, inspire; power from the center of the Earth
Below	Gen	quiet mountain; standing still, confidence rises from proper behavior.
The wisdom		Accomplishing small things Will clear the path. Largesse of compassion Balances frugality.

The essence of this hexagram, Xiao Guo, advises that as you proceed on the path toward your ideals, the benefit is to move with small, careful, exacting steps. The smallest of details are now of utmost importance.

Anything you've left for another day needs to be attended to now. Deal with old debts, either in-kind or financial, honestly. Be cautious, exacting, and frugal. In this way your resources will remain strong and intact for the larger movements that are coming your way.

> This is a solo journey.
> Do not look outside yourself
> Or depend on others to do the work for you.
> You can do this.

By being diligent while carefully considering each of the myriad small details, you can complete the tasks that lie before you on both the inner and outer planes. As you undertake the task of looking at the smallest of details, the sheer volume may feel overwhelming. The way here is to not make any one thing an uppermost priority. The tasks are numerous and may seem unconnected, but you will find that they are connected and are all a part of a whole. Simply take the first one that appears and deal with it, then the next, and so on, until you have made your way through the tangled jungle that has kept you captive.

In these efforts, consider the projects and ideas you've put on hold for another day and put them up against the template of truth, experience, and reality. In this way you will see what will work and what you should discard. The sense of relief from this house-cleaning will fill you with satisfaction and will activate your energy, which will be pleasant and sustaining. In this way you will please your spirits of inner guidance and make way for growth and maturity. Yet as good as you may feel from this exercise, refrain from any big actions or announcements, for at this time they would be disastrous.

This is the time to fly under the radar, moving toward your goal with little obvious motion. It is decidedly not a time to look for a grand hurrah from the tribe, community, well-wishers, associates, or lovers. Instead, stay steady in your efforts, and be organized and efficient. Know that you are in flight to a better day, a better year. Be respectful of the elders and teachers in your life. This will bring merit to you on this sacred journey on the wings of Spirit. The key is *offering:* you don't have to accept all that the Yi Jing teaches, however, should you refuse at this delicate time of humility and grace you would lose the opportunity for a subtle kind of growth and maturation, no matter what chronological age you are.

The architecture of this hexagram when laid on its side symbolizes a flying bird. You are the bird, and in this work you are vulnerable and could be a target of avarice or jealousy. The metaphor of flying low to the ground is vital. By doing so, with your eyes wide open, you will find the details that when attended to will keep you safe from judgment and attack. This position is not a passive one, for it is by being on top of all the little details that you can shift the energy a little bit at a time, poco a poco.

During this time the ego will want to have its way with you and convince you to fly higher and spread your wings and go for it. Here consider the story of Icarus, whose father, Daedalus, fashioned wings made of feathers and wax so he and his son could fly—and they did. Daedalus warned his son not to fly too close to the sun. Then the voice of his ego said to Icarus, "Fly higher, you can fly all the way to the sun and you will be a god." Icarus went higher and higher toward the sun and his wings melted from the heat of the sun and he fell into the sea, never accomplishing his goal of free flight.

Xian Guo counsels us to know that true and lasting strength will be gained from being attentive to the seemingly minor aspects of life. It's not glamorous, but you will benefit and find strength from taking time in stillness and attending to the needs of others. Put your attention on being of service; you may not be recognized for all you do and have done for others, but your efforts at being kind, caring, charitable, loving, and steady will put you in alignment with the chorus of souls who are in service to the transformation of global consciousness.

Challenging situations like this would not have come to you had you not been called to this test before achieving the glory of transformation. If in this stirring of the soul were you to react with anger or go into fear and doubt, you would miss a great opportunity for the transformative leap that was written in your soul contract. Pay no heed if the ego tells you that you aren't good enough. That is simply not true; by coming as far as you have, it shows that you have done well, and if you were not good enough you would certainly not be standing on this precipice of satisfying the soul. By making effort in small things, you acknowledge the completion of a cycle and pave the way for harmonizing with your family, community, friends, and associates.

Be steady. Renew your commitment to the natural world and all her beings. Talk less, listen more. Hear the rustle of the trees, the chattering of the birds, the whisper of the wind, and the melody of moving waters. In listening without judgment or agenda, you will hear and feel the inner voice of the ever-present sage, your sacred guidance. Accept this time with grace and dignity. Stay in the knowingness of your heart. Don't give up even on the smallest task. You are in a position to achieve your desires when your movements are modest, compassionate, and considerate of the whole.

63. JI JI ALREADY CROSSING

䷾

Above	Kan	gorge, precipice, taking risks
Below	Li	radiance, fire

The wisdom

You are approaching a great crossing,
A turning point in life.
You're looking good;
Humility denotes freedom.

You are now approaching a new and favorable cycle where your diligence will show up on the positive side of the ledger. You are at a crossing point. This is an exciting time, for it is from here that you can see across to the other shore and all that awaits you there. That which you have been working for, dreamed of, and kept in your heart is in view, and you can feel it. This is good. The challenge is to not let your ego push you too fast or too far in these delicate moments before realizing your goals, whether in love, business, or spirit.

In the Yi Jing, an early version of the I Ching, there is a parable that contains the teaching of this hexagram:

Once there was a wise old fox who in early spring stood at the edge of a great river that had frozen in winter. The old fox contemplated crossing, for on the other side were many things of wonder and delight—ample mice to chase and eat, many playful female foxes to entice him, and a warm den, prepared by his skulk, awaiting his arrival. The old fox contemplated the frozen river and its ice, waiting for the right time to cross. As the old fox stood on the banks of the river in contemplation, a brash young fox came bounding up to him. The young fox also knew what lay across the river, for he had heard the elders speak of this time of year when excitement and initiation awaited on the other shore. The young fox saw the old fox and said, "Old fox, what are you doing? Come, let's go across the river. There is much joy and comfort that awaits us." The old fox said nothing and continued to observe the river. The young fox said, "Well, if you won't come with me, too bad for you," and without a fare-thee-well began to head across the ice to the other side. The wise old fox said calmly and quietly, "Be careful, the ice is very thin in many places, it is not yet time to cross." As the young fox began to cross, a crack in the ice occurred midway, and the young fox fell through the ice, and had to make his way back in the freezing water to where the old fox still stood on the shore. While the young fox stood there shaking and trembling, soaked to the bone, the old fox waited until the sun started to go down and the frozen ice hardened, allowing him to handily cross over to the other side.

Take this story to heart now and do not become enamored with how well you have done getting to where you stand, lusting for what awaits you. Your destiny is on the other side, so use caution and embrace the teaching of old fox.

This tale informs you as to what all your planning, angst, and sleepless nights have been about: preparation. You are well-positioned now to achieve your goals. As you complete one cycle, a new one awaits, so be alert. It is in the natural order of things that once something is born, it grows, matures, serves its purpose, finishes its cycle, and dies, turning into a rich compost to feed the next cycle that is just across the river.

> This is not a time for arrogance or complacency.
> Look closely at what you have gleaned from

difficult times.
Integrate them as wisdom teachings.
In this way you will remain strong and resistant to decay.

Much is well-placed and in order in your life. The rights of passage that are before you now are vital on your quest for higher consciousness, love, and abundance. You can have it all, but it is imperative that you remain calm, centered, and find stillness each day as you do the work and balance it with rest, fun, and celebration, and gratitude for how far you've come. During the journey to get here you've learned how to use certain tools that have allowed you to stay on the mark. Whether it is meditation, walking, gardening, dancing, or some inner activity, stay with it. We human beings tend to achieve our goals and then forget how we got there, through focus and discipline. This is a time to remain diligent to what is right for you and for the greater good. You didn't get here on your own, there are invisible helpers active on behalf of each of us at all times. We just need to show our humility for this kind of support by surrendering to it in gratitude. In this way it will always be there for us on the road less traveled.

Pay heed to the life patterns you have recognized, dropped, or modified during this past cycle. Take a careful inventory as you enter the next cycle. With a still mind and a heart filled with gratefulness and love, recognize that you are forever changed, and you can now accomplish your dreams and desires.

Life consists of an endless round of cycles, whether we are ready for them or not. These life cycles have their own periodicity, their own time and agenda. Just as summer does not wait for spring, so it is with our cyclic nature. The new cycle has already begun.

It is in the nature of completion that there tends to be a minute area where decay can begin to form. This hexagram contains a caveat: we must be constantly vigilant so that we don't repeat old patterns, thought forms, or activities that would cause decay to take root. If we fall back into dysfunctional patterns, the fallout would carry over into the next cycle, and then we would have to repeat some not-so-pleasant feelings, heartache, or illness. So how you handle this transition will influence the coming tide. And the coming round will be toward being even more who you truly are—in your work, your relationships, and your inner and outer well-being.

Be in magnificent gratitude and wear it as a magical cape that moves you forward and protects you as you love and let yourself be loved. Take a moment and bless this day you have been given. Be grateful for eyes that see, ears that hear, and for the body, mind, and consciousness that is a gift of human incarnation.

64. WEI JI CORRECT ORDER/MISSING PIECES

䷿

Above Li — radiance, fire; brightness that brings clarity and passion

Below Kan — gorge, precipice, snare; taking risks; the danger of swift-flowing waters

The wisdom

All the proper pieces are present,
Yet there is something out of phase.
It will become clear.
Stand strong, protect the castle.

Success is imminent, there is no doubt. There is a new archetype forming that awaits subtle, creative movements to insure success. Be calm and organize. As well, be considerate as the existing pattern undergoes a major shift; anything inconsiderate at this time is dangerous. Above all, rely on traditional wisdom.

This kua is also called the Great Crossing. Consider, as is told in Chinese folklore, that you are about to cross a wide river. You can see that there are rocks that have been carefully placed, which you can use as stepping stones to make it safely to the other side. The other side represents success in the venture or situation in which you find yourself. It could be a business relationship, a system you have adhered to, or a process that is beneficial to your growth and to the attainment of what you have seen as beneficial. Consider each step as you gracefully cross the great divide.

The lesson is clear: pay close attention in order to recognize the proper timing, and make sure your plan is fully formed; then make your move.

There have been beneficial advances on your journey. The temptation now is to tell yourself, *Let's get this done! It's been too long in the waiting!* But to move fast, you would not be surefooted on each step across the great river. There must be a considered plan. This is not hard once the ego is put in its place and you do not respond to its demands. You have great influence now on the way across; make your plan and stick to it.

> Your passion to advance is triggering a hormonal rush.
> All seems possible, and it is.
> Cool the ego;
> Take stock of the situation and proceed with due consideration.

The benefit now is to be sure that what you have done in preparation for this change is in proper order. Look closely. Tame the inner chaos, and gather the emotional, spiritual, and psychological food you need for the journey ahead. Then all depends on correct timing; be still and listen inwardly so that you will recognize the right time to make your move.

You have been in similar situations before. Consider the lessons you have learned, and with compassion release situations, agreements, and people that have held you—and that you have held—in the bondage of old programs and patterns. This will leave you feeling free and light of spirit; you will have released the weight that has kept you from what your heart desires and what you are here in this life to create and complete.

In reward for the work you've done you now have an opportunity to ride a powerful energetic wave. This wave fuels your connection to the Divine and to the universal source of wisdom.

Note well: you have been sent in the right direction, to the right place at the right time, almost as if you had no choice in the matter. Trust that this guidance is your inner knowing operating at its finest vibration and highest frequency. This realization is vital when it comes to trusting your intuition and allowing you to love without conditions and to advance with an open, nonjudgmental consciousness.

Walk your path with dignity, compassion, kindness, and integrity. In this way you are caring for your soul as you move smoothly toward a new, creative beginning. Come to an agreement with yourself that you will trust your intuitive knowing. The resulting message will be clear and in a language that is familiar. You will need no translator, shrink, shaman, or priest to tell you what is being said; rather, you will know it from the subtle voice of your own inner wisdom. It is this voice that got you here, to stand at the gates of destiny, fully exposed. Have no fear, you are on time, in time.

A rebirth and a new beginning awaits you. Close the old chapters and cut off the dead weight with a sharp, swift sword. Releasing negative thought forms will free you from the bondage of control by those patterns that are no longer appropriate, and from associations, relationships, and agreements that are no longer valid.

On the horizon there are new people, exciting possibilities, and new endeavors. You will be rich with new ideas and be received by welcoming souls of like mind and purpose. Trust the process and listen to your heart. Quiet the analytical mind's voice of doubt.

There is peace in every step.

ACKNOWLEDGMENTS

So many souls have helped and inspired me to write this book.

First, in gratitude for my incredible editor, Margret Jones, whose brilliance and belief in me have been fuel to the passionate fire of my work.

To the teachers and mentors who have blessed me on my journey, my heartfelt thanks: my Tai Chi master Marshall Ho'; my Hopi teachers Mina Lansa, Grandfather David Monongye, and Thomas Banyakya, who opened the doors at Oriabe to me to learn with the spiritual keepers of wisdom for our planet; and my Jungian teacher and therapist, Dr. Malcom Boyd Dana, who taught me the way in caring for my soul.

I also make a dedication to my children Justine and Jake, who have been great teachers in challenging times. And lastly, to my oldest friend, the great artist Joby Baker, who with biting humor and great love helped keep me real, with my head in the clouds and feet on the ground.

Photo Anna Fishkin

ABOUT BOBBY KLEIN

Bobby Klein, PhD, is a clinical psychologist, multidimensional healer, meditation instructor, and psycho-spiritual counselor with an international clientele. His method uses sacred technologies involving light and sound and calls on universal synchronistic guidance to open the heart and mind and explore expanded consciousness. Following a stint in the late sixties as a photographer for the Doors, Janis Joplin, and other pop-culture figures, he studied acupuncture and oriental medicine and was influential in bringing it into widespread acceptance in the United States. After forty years in Los Angeles where he had a successful private practice, he moved to Tulum, Mexico, where he founded the Yäan Wellness Energy Spa. In addition to continuing his private practice in Tulum, he holds retreats there and around the world that focus on opening the heart to Spirit and taking the journey of remembering one's authentic self.